Rock
What
You've
Got

Katherine Schwarzenegger

Rock
What
You've
Got

secrets to
loving your
inner and outer
beauty

from someone
who's been
there and back

voice
HYPERION | NEW YORK

Library of Congress Cataloging-in-Publication Data has been applied for. ISBN: 978-1-4013-4143-5

Hyperion books are available for special promotions and premiums. For details contact the HarperCollins Special Markets Department in the New York office at 212-207-7528, fax 212-207-7222, or email spsales@harpercollins.com.

Design by Dopodomani

FIRST EDITION

10 9 8 7 6 5 4 3 2 1

Dedication

To Mom and Dad for all of the love and encouragement you have poured into me throughout my life. I cherish the support and advice you've both shared throughout the journey I've taken with this book. You have been the best parents and teachers I could have ever asked for. I'm forever grateful to have you in my life.

To my sister, Christina, and brothers, Patrick and Christopher, for providing me with stories and experiences that not only helped me write this book but also helped make me the person I am today. I appreciate all your support and love.

To my extended family and friends, for loving me and accepting me through all my shapes and sizes.

And to every girl who has been embarrassed by her body and doubted her worth as a human being: May you always remember to own and love what God gave you. And most of all, may you learn to **Rock What You've Got.**

Contents

Rock
What
You've
Got

Only **2** percent of women describe themselves as beautiful.

63 percent of women surveyed strongly agree that society expects women to enhance their physical attractiveness.

45 percent of all women feel women who are more beautiful have greater opportunities in life.

68 percent of women strongly agree that the media and advertising set an unrealistic standard of beauty that most women can't ever achieve.

76 percent wish female beauty was portrayed in the media as being made up of more than just physical attractiveness.

75 percent of women say they wish the media did a better job of portraying women of diverse physical attractiveness, including age, shape, and size.

Source: 2004 Dove Study, "Only Two Percent of Women Describe Themselves As Beautiful: New Global Study Uncovers Desire for Broader Definition of Beauty."

"I hate myself!"

I cried to my mother.

"I'm fat, I'm ugly, I'm stupid, and I feel totally disgusting!" I was only ten years old and in the fourth grade, and already suffering, but this was the first time I could recall revealing my worries about my appearance to anyone.

I shared my prepubescent misery with my family on a flight from Los Angeles to Sun Valley, Idaho, where we were headed for a weekend getaway. I didn't want to go on the trip because I had my first lengthy report due for school, and I was totally nervous about it. This was the first time I had a homework assignment that completely overwhelmed me. The dreaded fourteen-page "Nobel Report" struck fear in the hearts of kids in the lower grades, who knew that when they reached fourth grade they would finally be assigned this project. My brain was on overload. I was tired, feeling insecure, and downright mad about having to go on the trip. By the time our plane took off, I was headed for a full-on meltdown.

Clearly, how I looked on the outside was only part of the issue when it came to how I was feeling on the inside. I used my frustration to vent all of the pent-up unfamiliar feelings I was having about myself. I was terrified of my fourth grade teacher, and I was doing awful in school for the first time. I was being challenged in my classes in ways I had never been before. Whenever I raised my hand to ask a question about something that confused me, I could hear the other kids in my class, mostly the boys, snicker and call me names.

"How could she not know that?" I'd hear one boy say while another would cough out the word *stupid*.

My reaction to their comments was to fake a sudden understanding of the lesson that had been confusing me and hope the teacher would just move on.

Now, for those of you who don't know my parents, my mother, Maria Shriver, comes from a very powerful and competitive family. She has been successful throughout her life as a top TV journalist and bestselling author, and is currently first lady of California. Of course, my father is Arnold Schwarzenegger, the governor of California and bodybuilding champion, and yes, he was the Terminator!

He is also a former Mr. Universe and Mr. Olympia, two titles he earned as a champion bodybuilder. But to me, they're just "Mom" and "Dad." Despite their fame and success, I grew up in a pretty normal home, dealing with issues that all families contend with. Sometimes we disagreed with one another, but our home life was always filled with love, compassion, and understanding.

My mom was especially concerned about us growing up in Los Angeles because she didn't want us to become spoiled Hollywood kids. Given our unique family circumstances, she worked hard to give us as normal an upbringing as possible, teaching us to be good kids, to respect them as parents, to show respect to others, to be grateful, polite, appreciative, and educated about money, to stay down-to-earth, and to give back to our community.

Looking back, I can genuinely say that I am truly grateful that my parents sheltered us from the public eye. This may sound like an easy task, but it was probably the hardest thing they had to figure out as parents—how to give their kids a normal childhood even though they were always in the spotlight. And the fact that we all had a very recognizable last name didn't make their job any easier.

Both of my parents grew up feeling very confident, with a strong *sense of self-worth,* gifts they were doing their best to pass on to my three younger siblings and me. A self-defeating attitude, pity parties, and self-loathing aren't a part of their worlds, and it wasn't how they were raising their children.

Whenever I told my mom *I didn't feel smart,* she assured me that I was a bright and intelligent girl. If I told her I felt ugly, she'd tell me I was beautiful. When I told her I was miserable, she'd remind me how blessed I am. My mom had a way of knowing how to turn my negative statements into positive ones, something I had yet to learn. I knew she said things like that to comfort me, but it didn't always make me feel better because, well, let's face it, *she* is *my* mom. She's *supposed* to say those things to me, right? I actually believed it was her responsibility to tell me stuff like I am beautiful when I feel unattractive or that I am not fat when I think I am. I thought all moms did and said things like that to get their daughters through the awkward years. After all, they were once young like us too. But I realize now that not all mothers say these things to their daughters, and it *is* a big deal.

When my younger sister, Christina, and I were babies, my mother constantly reminded us that we had to be more in life than just a pretty face. My father took a videotape of us sitting in our high chairs saying aloud, "I'm beautiful, smart, nice, and kind . . ." over and over with hand motions to go along with it. It's a little embarrassing to look at now, but it was the start of building our self-confidence and self-esteem.

With that kind of support and positive reinforcement growing up, it may seem strange that I was suddenly feeling so much doubt and insecurity. Admittedly, I consider fourth grade to be one of my "chubby" years as a kid. I felt overweight, and looking back at old pictures of myself, I can honestly say I wasn't fat, but I certainly felt that way.

Up until then, I was always pencil thin. Without warning and with little awareness that it was happening, my body had changed. I was no longer the skinny little girl I had always been. In fact, the changes were so unexpected that I thought something must be wrong because I was inexplicably gaining weight.

I wasn't eating any differently than I used to.

I wasn't going through puberty . . . yet.

My body just changed, which I wasn't ready or properly prepared to face.

As we reached our cruising altitude on the flight to Idaho that day, I was now all out sobbing. Instead of comforting me, my mom took out a pad of paper and a pen. She drew a line down the center of the paper and wrote "Likes" and "Don't Likes" at the top of each column. She asked me to list all of the things I liked about myself and then the things I didn't. I had to really stop and think about the things I liked.

I paused.

And then I yelled, "I don't like anything!" My sobs turned into uncontrollable weeping—you know the kind of crying where you can't catch a breath.

"I hate myself and I feel ugly all the time." I could barely get the words out of my mouth.

My mom continued to calmly walk me through a series of questions, focusing on all of my assets instead of my perceived flaws.

"Do you like your hair or hate your hair?" Mom asked.

"I like my hair, I guess," I replied in between breathless gasps and streaming tears.

"Do you like your eyes or hate your eyes?"

"I like those too," I said.

She made me write each of these attributes in the "Likes" column. One by one, we made a list of all the things I actually felt good about instead of what made me feel insecure. It was obvious there was more bothering me than just my looks. I was just too young to articulate all of the conflict I was feeling at the time.

After I calmed down, I was able to explain to my mother that I was angry because I didn't think I was as smart as the other kids in school. The classes in my school were divided up into slow, average, and advanced groups. When it came to math, I was in the slow class. This distinction and separation from most of my friends was eating away at my self-esteem. It made me feel isolated and "different." Looking back, I now realize the system our school implemented wasn't in the students' best interests, but at the time, it solidified my self-belief that I was not smart—and that really hurt.

I explained to my mother that math was the class I felt worst about. I told her how the teacher made me feel like a complete idiot for not understanding the problems.

"I was never very good at math, Katherine, but that didn't make me stupid or stop me from achieving my goals. You're not stupid, honey, you're really smart," my mother reassuringly said. "I became successful without being perfect at math, and you can too."

By the time the pilot announced we were landing, I remarkably realized that there were a lot more "Likes" about myself than "Dislikes" on the lists my mom and I had made during the flight. I felt better about myself than I had in months and actually began to look forward to a couple of days away from the pressures of school and life, not to mention spending some quality time skiing with my family.

Despite my mom's effort to show me I wasn't any of those negative things I was feeling, those old self-doubts reappeared shortly after we returned to Los Angeles. When I went back to school, my temporary feeling of being at ease disappeared and my old feelings of insecurity returned. Old habits are hard to break, even in the fourth grade. And once you've accepted those beliefs to be the truth, they are easy to indulge in and become reinforced. I spent the next several years of my life fighting my constant self-doubt. I felt like I was losing my mind.

Was I depressed?

No.

Was there something horribly wrong?

Not that I could put my finger on.

So why was I feeling this way?

It turns out that ***I was a typical struggling preteen.***

Most of my feelings were completely and totally age appropriate and normal. Of course, I now know that all girls struggle with the onset of adolescence, but at the time I really thought I was the only girl in the entire world who felt bad about herself. And as I got older, my problems only seemed to get harder to handle, especially the perception I had of my weight and, in turn, my body image.

By the time I entered seventh grade, **all the rules had changed.** I found the new atmosphere even more challenging. There were a lot more kids in middle school, the classes were held on a different campus than the lower school classes, and we were the awkward "new" kids on campus trying to find our way.

It was hard to make new friends, especially because there were a lot more kids who recognized my very distinctive last name.

"Are you *Arnold's* daughter?" they'd say, as if it were some big deal. It wasn't to me, but then again, not everyone's dad was the Terminator, right? It was awkward to study American history and read a whole chapter on my mother's family. My heritage was something that I couldn't escape, and it made me terribly self-conscious and insecure.

As I got older, I was adamant about keeping the friends I knew from elementary school, the kids who liked me for me, because I was worried the new kids in middle and high school only wanted to be friends because of who my parents are. This was something I worried about, perhaps unnecessarily so, at least until I discovered boys. That's when it became obvious who was interested in me and who was more interested in my dad.

A few short days into middle school, I was faced with my first official body image dilemma in our physical education class. Because I attended private school, all of the kids were required to wear uniforms for PE. I vividly remember all of us girls standing in the locker room, gym clothes in hand, nearly frozen, waiting to see who would be the first to undress. Some girls just took off their clothes and changed while others headed straight to the bathroom stalls to have privacy. For the first time in my life, I was really nervous about what the other girls would think—or worse, possibly say out loud—when they saw my body. I slowly removed my pants so I could quickly slip on my gym shorts, hoping and praying no one was looking. Despite my best Houdini-esque quick change, I felt as if a thousand sets of eyes were watching me as I undressed, making mental notes of everything wrong with my body. It was painfully awkward.

I remember hearing some older girls in the locker room at school that year staring in the mirror and talking about their bodies.

"I hate my legs," one said.

"What are you talking about? Your legs are perfect. Have you seen how big my hips are?" another commented.

"Ugh! My arms are so fat," said a third girl.

Their critical statements were puzzling to me because *I thought they all looked perfect.* I couldn't see what they were looking at when they talked about themselves. I wondered why these very pretty girls were picking apart their bodies as if they each had giant humpbacks, three eyes, or other gross and irreparable flaws. If I had overheard girls saying things like that about someone else, I would have thought they were just being mean. Instead, these girls were picking on themselves, not others.

Until I overheard that exchange, my only thought about body image had been whether someone was fat or skinny. These girls were zeroing in on their bodies in ways I had never considered, critically analyzing each detail of various body parts. They ripped apart every little flaw. That was the beginning of my own critical self-examination and hyper-awareness of my body.

I went home that afternoon and stood in front of the mirror in my underwear for what seemed like hours. I carefully studied my body from head to toe, noticing every flaw, imperfection, and detail that looked "wrong," "out of place," or "unappealing" to me. I looked long and hard until it suddenly became clear that yes, I was flat chested, which I thought looked totally weird on my body frame. I was horrified I didn't have boobs yet, since most of my friends were more developed. One good friend was already wearing a D cup, which I envied. I'd look in the mirror and wonder, "Where are they?"

A lot of my girlfriends had long skinny legs that looked like two toothpicks. They pranced around in bathing suits with thighs that never moved. My legs were not as thin or firm as theirs. I stood in front of the mirror, jiggling my legs. I gasped after noticing a lot of action in my thighs. I also didn't think my sandy-colored hair was as beautiful as the lighter shade of California blond all my friends had. I had tons of freckles that ran across my too pointy nose, my shoulders were bony, and my hips seemed to be spreading at an alarming rate. I hated everything I discovered in the mirror that night.

Everything.

> _I try not to weigh myself. As long as I fit in my jeans, I'm good. It's so easy to become obsessed with a number on a scale! It's a slippery slope, and pretty soon, you'll be weighing yourself all the time, and for what?_
>
> **—BETSY, RICHMOND, VIRGINIA**

It was official. I had become one of "those" girls I saw in the locker room earlier that day. I suddenly realized that life would never be the same again.

From that day on, I became obsessed with weighing myself—and I mean all the time. I feared going to the doctor's office for my annual checkup, panicked at the thought of the big black weight on the scale shifting from fifty to one hundred pounds. My mother had the same type of medical scale in her bathroom as in the pediatrician's office. I'd sometimes purposely shower in her room so I could secretly weigh myself, sometimes twice a day, hoping and praying I hadn't gained any weight since my weigh-in the day before. I was mortified thinking about triple digits on the scale.

The struggle with my body image and self-esteem continued well into high school. I took a sex education class my freshman year that taught us about the changes girls' bodies go through as they mature into women. It sounded horrible! Wide hips, big boobs (which I then viewed as nothing more than two welts of fat), bigger butts, and even larger thighs! Based on that less-than-appealing description, I thought the next few years would be a living hell.

I made it through middle school maintaining a constant weight of 95 to 98 pounds. I was determined to stay under 100 pounds until I went to high school—and I did. I started ninth grade weighing in at what I believed to be a hefty 101 pounds and feeling horrible, like I was a fat blob. My immediate reaction was to skip my next meal and starve myself until I dropped two pounds to get my weight under 100 pounds.

Even though most people would have told you I was thin, I had finally teetered over the 100-pound mark on the scale. It didn't take long for the scale to creep back up over that dreaded mark. I now weighed a staggering 108! Ugh. This was when I began experimenting with every fad diet known to man. I tried my hardest to starve myself, but nothing I was doing seemed to work. ***I hated my body.***

Growing up, our home was always filled with lots of activity and action. My father is an avid workout fanatic. He still finds the time to exercise twice a day, even as the governor, with a crazy work schedule! My mom exercises religiously every day too. Their active lifestyle was passed on to my two younger brothers, Patrick and Christopher, my sister, Christina, and me. We were never allowed to sit around and veg out in front of the television or play video games all day. If the sun was out, we were outside playing a game or doing something active. Growing up in Southern California had certain advantages, such as the weather, which allowed us to spend the majority of our free time after school and on the weekends doing things outdoors. We played tennis, biked, hiked, and I got to ride horses.

Summer vacations were no exception to the rule. My parents always made sure we did something useful with our time. According to my parents, summer was not a time to relax or take a break from the everyday routine of going to school; it was a time to get ahead and do something useful and meaningful with our time. When I was younger, I played sports and went to camp. As I got older, my parents began to instill in us the importance of giving back to the community, especially those places around the world that are less fortunate than my very privileged life growing up in Los Angeles.

At the end of ninth grade, my parents agreed to send me to Costa Rica to participate in a community service exchange program, where we would live with a family, learn Spanish, and do work in the community. This was my first trip out of the country on my own. The home-stay family I lived with owned a dairy farm. The father often pointed over to a cow and told me in Spanish, "You see that one over there? She will be good for dinner tonight." The thought of eating that cow later on freaked me out. If they served hamburgers, I couldn't eat, because all I could see on my plate was the face of that poor cow, which had been a living, breathing animal in the pasture just a few hours earlier. The only other thing left on the dinner table to eat was bread, so I'd fill up on that before anyone could notice I wasn't eating the meat, which might have been taken as rude or disrespectful.

During my three weeks there, my diet was mainly warm, fresh baked homemade bread and tortillas. I couldn't resist the temptation every time a new loaf came out of the oven. My carefree eating brought me home, give or take, fifteen to twenty pounds heavier than when I left. I wasn't immediately aware of my rapid and drastic weight gain because I mostly wore baggy sweats with an elastic waist or drawstring tie and big T-shirts while I was there. Since I primarily wore loose-fitting workout clothes, it was easy to be oblivious to my quickly expanding waistline. Plus, my height of five feet eight inches gives me the added advantage of being able to carry around a few extra pounds, which someone else who is shorter simply can't pull off as well.

It wasn't until I came home and tried to slip into my favorite pair of jeans that my changed body became obvious and appalling all at once. Although I wanted to believe that someone must have shrunk my jeans while I was away, the harsh reality was that my pants didn't get smaller—I had gotten bigger!

Sometime during my first days back in Los Angeles, one of my best girlfriends came to my house to hear all about my trip. When I opened the front door, I heard her say, "Wow! You look so . . . healthy!"

"Healthy? What does that mean?" I wondered aloud.

My friend stumbled for an appropriate answer, but there wasn't one.

"Um . . . You look, I don't know, just healthy."

That's when I knew for sure that what she meant was that **I looked FAT.**

I spent tenth grade struggling to lose the extra weight it took me less than a month to gain. I tried starving myself and working out like I was a girl on a mission. I worked my butt off that whole year to get back to my skinny middle school self, but my body never fully got back to what it used to be. I had to accept and realize that I would never be *that* girl again.

I hated my body, and worse than that, I actually believed there was nothing I could do to change how I felt—helpless, confused, and mad at myself because I had no one to blame but myself for allowing myself to gain all of that weight in the first place.

Looking back, I can now laugh at myself for thinking that I actually believed my problems were unique—singular to little ol' me. I spent years stressed-out and full of angst, trying to be the image of what I believed everyone else thought I should look like. I wasted so many years chasing perfection, wallowing in self-doubt and torturing myself, all of which made me miss out on some of the best years of my life.

Over what?

A few extra pounds!

Learning to love my inner and outer beauty wasn't an easy road. I still don't always love the reflection I see in the mirror, but I have learned that my outer appearance does not define me. I still get mad when I put on my jeans and they are a little bit tight or if I put on a dress that fits differently than it did a month ago when I bought it. But I don't go into a tailspin. I now know and appreciate that I can be **confident** in my skin regardless of my dress size. I have many other great qualities that define me other than my weight on a scale.

SECRET . . . STOP STRESSING!

1 Fitness experts say *not to weigh yourself more than once a week.* I recommend weighing yourself once a month to give your body a chance to regulate. Your weight on a scale can fluctuate between five pounds, depending on what you've had to eat that day, your salt intake, when you've gone to the bathroom, etc. You can't let that number dictate how you feel on any given day. *So, stop stressing!*

I spent years allowing one singular flaw here and there to cast a gigantic shadow over all of the good blessings I had in life. I have great friends, a loving and supportive family, a passion for riding, and lots of personal interests in philanthropy that I was and still am passionate about. Then I had my first real, what I like to call an Oprah "A-ha" realization, one that led me to finally embrace the insight that yes, ***I am a curvy, powerful, smart, confident, loving, sexy, and happy woman.*** Let me be clear. For me this did not happen overnight. It took a couple of years for me to sit and embrace my body as it is.

I was finally able to accept that I will never be stick thin again and that I was blessed to have a curvier figure, so I should love it and embrace it.

I will most likely never be one of the cover girl models I see on magazines with a perfect body and flawless skin and long flowing, shiny, never-frizzy hair.

Nope.

But that's okay with me because I have also realized that I no longer have to measure myself against those girls to feel and be beautiful. As long as I eat right, exercise, and continue to live healthfully, I am just as good as any supermodel!

It took ten years of struggling with my self-image and self-esteem to come to a place of understanding, acceptance, and self-love for my body and myself, regardless of my dress size, and to not only understand this message but also to finally stop listening to my inner critic.

My journey of how I got here is what ultimately led me to wanting to share my experiences with you in this book. I've been through the various problems, issues, and concerns you are now facing or will face in the future.

Even if you feel like you're the only girl in the world who is suffering, I assure you that you're not.

I've been there.
I've struggled.

I've cried alone in my bedroom at night. I woke up in the morning filled with angst about going to school. I've stood in front of the mirror and wanted to scream about how I looked. I've been embarrassed to go outside in a bikini. I've heard the cruel commentary from the boys and girls in the cafeteria or the back of the classroom about my weight or dumb questions.

And guess what?

I lived through it all, and so will you!

In fact, someday you may even look back on all of the

drama you're now fighting and laugh about it, like I do. It may not seem possible now, but it's true. Believe me, when I came home from Costa Rica twenty pounds heavier, it wasn't funny.

Nope.

Not even a little bit.

But now, just a few years later, my girlfriends and I laugh about it. I can look at my best friend, who said I came home "healthy," and say, "Did I ever look in the mirror when I was there? How could I not notice an extra twenty pounds?" and just laugh.

The gift of laughter is the best tool you can arm yourself with throughout these turbulent and awkward years.

I know. Easier said than done, right?

But if you can find the humor in the absurd daily struggles, if you can laugh at others' irritating remarks, if you can learn not to take every little thing so seriously, if you can learn to allow your inner beauty to work its way outward, those awful feelings will eventually slip away, and you will not only survive, you will thrive.

Happiness isn't found in being emaciated, having flawless skin, or supermodel legs that never end. We can only gain true happiness by loving ourselves, our inner and outer beauty, for all that we are and even for those things that we are not—or as I have defined it, learning to

Rock What You've Got!

Look in the Mirror.

Girls spend a lot of time with this.

You can make it your best friend or

your worst enemy.

CHAPTER 1

Mirror, Mirror, on the Wall

your *body* image

FACT

The average fashion model is over six feet tall and weighs well under 120 pounds. The average American woman is five feet four inches and weighs 140 pounds. Less than 5 percent of all women have the body type they see in magazines. So QUIT STRESSING OVER IT!

> *I hear women say that they are big and beautiful, but I honestly think that if they had the chance, they would be thin in a minute!*
>
> **—KIMBERLY M., ATLANTA, GEORGIA**

FACT

According to the National Mental Health Information Center, girls are three times more likely than boys to have a negative body image.

Body image is how a person views her physical self. A *Rock What You've Got* girl is a girl who has a positive body image, doesn't talk negatively about herself or others, eats food that is healthful, has consideration for other people's feelings, doesn't let people treat her poorly, and knows that she won't always make everyone happy or like her, so she is content with knowing she likes herself.

Our body image is heightened as we mature from adolescent girls to young women. This is a critical time in a girl's life because it is when most girls begin to care about how they look, not just to others but also to themselves. This obsession starts as early as middle school and, for some girls, even sooner.

Sometime during these adolescent and teen years, young girls become so concerned with their body image that it takes over most other aspects of their lives. A girl with a negative body image often talks negatively about herself and others, chooses to do whatever she wants regardless of the consequences, has little or no integrity, rarely finishes anything she starts, doesn't take care of her physical health, allows her friends to treat her poorly, and constantly looks to others for approval. Some girls won't even participate in sports for fear their muscular bodies may become too thick or bulky, while others discover that working out is a great way to stay in shape, conditioning not only the outside but also your inside too, like your heart. But some girls can even become compulsive about their exercising. It's also very common for girls to become overly consumed about the clothes they wear and wanting to fit in and be like all the other girls in school.

I was a late bloomer in this department, mostly because I wore a uniform to school until the seventh grade. Around this time I started experimenting with fashion and caring about what I was wearing. Making the wrong choice about which outfit to wear might subject me to ridicule or rejection, which was just another opportunity to feel bad about myself. In an effort to avoid any unwanted embarrassment, I'd call my best girlfriends every morning and ask what they were wearing that day, to make sure I didn't stand out or look foolish. If they were going to wear their Juicy jumpsuits, I would make sure to wear mine too. Looking back, we must have looked like a walking advertisement, all dressed in identical outfits! I was never overly concerned with doing my hair or wearing lots of makeup, but I definitely started paying attention to my clothes.

Fashion is a cool way to project our personalities to others. It's also a way we enhance our "outer" beauty. We all have our "look." I have to confess that I wasn't sure how to describe my own style at first, so I asked a couple of friends what they thought. They said that my look is feminine, comfortable, classic, chic, and active.

What's yours? If you're not sure, ask your friends to help you.

If you can't come up with an answer to the style question, maybe you're too consumed with what everyone else is wearing and not what makes you . . . you! Every time you see someone and think "She looks great!" you are getting a glimpse into her personality. She's most likely projecting a confident outside presence because she feels really good about herself on the inside. That's a sure sign of someone who is comfortable with her body image.

We all know when we rock a favorite pair of jeans or dress. I know I do. When I wear a special outfit that I know looks really good, I feel better about myself. If I am wearing pants that are too tight or shoes that hurt my feet, I spend the entire time regretting that decision.

It's true that we will all suffer for the sake of fashion from time to time, but it is important to know that clothes do not define who you are. Trust me. Anyone who judges you on the designer label you're sporting (or not) isn't a friend. You may make the decision to wear designer clothes, but in the end, these won't make you more friends, won't guarantee a date with that special guy you've been eyeing, won't make you happier with the person you are on the inside. The only thing it will do is set you back financially.

Being fashionable is expensive, especially for young women. The media create an expectation that young women should dress a certain way, despite the costs associated with being current. This imperative can and often does lead to shoplifting, because some girls feel so desperate to fit in by wearing the "right" clothes that they'll go to any length to get them—even if it means they have to steal.

It's easy to be overwhelmed and stressed-out about how others may see you, or to feel like you don't measure up. But don't let that pressure consume your life. You can be just as hip and stylish in an outfit from H&M as you can in couture. It's about the way you wear the clothes, not the price tag!

> *In sixth grade, my class went on a week-long camping trip. When the counselors encouraged us to finish everything on the plate, a boy in my class turned to me and said, 'Oh, that won't be a problem for you!'*
>
> **—BETH, NEW YORK, NEW YORK**

It is common for girls to be judged by their appearance and therefore to feel pressure to measure up to the high expectations that have been set by all of the outside influences that contribute to a negative body image.

The truth is, if you are a five-foot-four-inch medium-build girl, you will never, ever be a five-foot-eleven waiflike supermodel.

It isn't possible.

So why do so many girls refuse to accept and love their body as is and aim for that anyway?

It may surprise you to know that the average American woman wears a size fourteen, though you wouldn't know it if you read fashion magazines, Hollywood tabloids, or watch television, where a size zero is the norm and size four is teetering on "overweight." Open just about any magazine, look at a billboard, watch a movie or television show, and notice the girls you see in the images being presented.

They appear to be perfect.

Only, they're not.

They've been nipped, tucked, capped, lasered, colored, cut, airbrushed, and Photoshopped to look that way. It's no wonder 98 percent of girls in America can't look at themselves and say they're beautiful. Really, when you think about it, why would we think we're beautiful when all we see every day in the media are images of drop-dead gorgeous women?

Sorry to be the bearer of bad news, but *perfection is impossible.*

" *I think it's a scandal, especially the emphasis on changing one's appearance with makeup, waxing, etc. (and that women who don't are unclean, unattractive, unfeminine, etc.). Luckily there has been a lot of awareness about the deceptions of Photoshop in ad campaigns, and perhaps that will have some effect on whether these women are perceived as representing a realistic body type.*

—NINA, NEW YORK, NEW YORK "

It's not real, but sadly **the chase is never-ending.**

It's a setup for failure!

We will all lose if outer beauty is the measure by which we gauge who we are in this world. And the scary truth is that girls as young as five years old are being negatively influenced by images they see on television and other outlets.

FIVE YEARS OLD!

This statistic should be of major concern to all of us.

A study conducted by the University of South Florida states that "nearly half of the three- to six-year-old participants fretted about being fat. About a third said they'd like to change their appearance—adopt a new hair color or lose weight."

Okay.

Stop.

Read that paragraph again.

I'm talking about three- to six-year-old girls feeling that way about their bodies!

That's insane!

Girls are increasingly growing dissatisfied with their bodies at an earlier age, trying to change them and fit into some image or mold of perfection that is impossible to achieve.

Where are they getting these messages from?

The answer is clear: their moms, sisters, friends, frenemies, television, movies, magazines, and every other media outlet imaginable.

It's a harsh reality that girls are more vulnerable to unrealistic beauty messages than boys are. We are especially self-critical, even when we don't mean to be. When you open a magazine or watch a movie, what kind of girls do you see?

Skinny ones!

Impossibly perfect girls with immaculate bodies.

Society tells us that looking good is not only attainable but also something that almost everyone wants. Think about it. How many times have you seen an ad in a magazine that touts the benefits of "longer, thicker lashes" or "glowing skin" or "bouncy, healthy, and shiny hair"? In fact, most cosmetic companies use celebrities to endorse their products these days in an effort to drive home the message that we can all look like our favorite movie star if we just use that product. And keep in mind they are *selling* a product, ladies, so they will promise you anything to get you to buy it. Most of these products don't actually deliver. They don't even work on the models that represent them. There is a team of stylists and makeup artists who make the model look the way she appears in an advertisement. So don't think one skin cream or hair product will transform you. ***If it sounds too good to be true, it probably is!***

It is absolutely normal to want to look good. The real question is: How will you get there?

The quest for the perfect body is not an easy one. In fact, it leaves most girls feeling frustrated, ashamed, and defeated with every failed attempt. These feelings can last a lifetime and will ultimately impact every area in a grown woman's life—from her career to her friendships and relationships to her overall happiness and contentment.

FACT

A 2002 Harvard University Press study revealed that "90 percent of teenage girls frequently talk about their body shape and that 86 percent of those girls think they should be dieting."

evolutionarily speaking, we are attracted to people with small waists or six-pack abs because that signals health. An emphasis on physical appearance has been around as long as history has been recorded, dating back at least to the time of the ancient Greeks, who viewed beautiful women as having higher social status. For centuries, heavyset women with really curvy bodies were adored and admired. Seventeenth-century artist Peter Paul Rubens loved to paint portraits of heavy nude women, as he and the culture he lived in found rounder women to be more desirable. A woman's girth was also a sign of wealth. The bigger she was, the more money she had.

corsets date back to the sixteenth century, but they weren't called "corsets" until the nineteenth century. Women wore these tightly laced undergarments to give them a much-desired hourglass shape. It's ironic that women today in the United States are heavier than ever—while there has never been more pressure on them to look thin.

there have been countless studies that show physically attractive people are thought to have more positive attributes than those who are not, by most standards, attractive. For example, physically attractive people are thought to have more outgoing personalities, to be more socially and professionally successful, and are generally thought to be more satisfied with their lives. But what makes a person "physically attractive"? One thing's for sure. It's **not** all about the perfect physique.

What if I asked you to put this book down, undress to your underwear, stand in front of a mirror, and take a good look at your body?

✔ **Does the mere thought of this freak you out?**
✔ **Does it fill you with panic-fueled anxiety?**
✔ **Would you be among the 86 percent of girls who think they need to be on a diet?**
✔ **And if you find the courage to actually look in a full-length mirror, what do you see?**

If your answer is yes to the first three questions, then you are not alone. That makes you like most girls, so this daunting but important exercise becomes anything but simple!

If you were to go through with it, most of you would stand there, spotting the tiniest flaws and the smallest imperfections that only YOU can see. There isn't a girl alive who hasn't stood in front of a mirror and said, "I'm sooooo fat!"

Even if you're a healthy, normal weight, most of you will probably look in that mirror and think you look fat and ugly. That's just wrong!

This endless pursuit of flawlessness has become a life-long cycle for so many. It starts when we are young girls and often follows us into womanhood. Sadly, once it starts, it's very difficult to break. Hard, but not impossible. All it takes is the courage to love the skin you're in and ***rock what you've got.***

exercise

This exercise is the same one my mom made me do on that flight to Sun Valley. It may seem elementary, but it will help you discover all of your assets, so just DO IT!

Divide a piece of paper in half. Write the words "Like" and "Dislike" at the top of two columns. Make a list of all the things you like and dislike about your appearance. When you finish, read your list out loud. How does it make you feel? More likes than you thought, huh?

NEWS FLASH!

This just in . . . *there is no such thing as a perfect body.*

I wish I could shout this from the highest mountaintop so every girl could hear that statement. Unfortunately, I am not much of a yodeler, so I'll have to trust that reading this will let you know how passionate I am about this subject.

Okay. So now that I've assured you there's no such thing as a perfect body, why do most of us believe there is?

I met Dr. Christiane Northrup a couple of years ago at the California Women's Conference. It wasn't a long encounter, but I never forgot our exchange. I asked her if she ever struggled with her body image. She said she had. I was curious how this world-renowned physician, a woman who inspires good health in girls of all ages, recovered from her own body image issues.

Dr. Northrup sort of smiled and said, "I started to recover at around age fifty-five!" I was stunned by her candid response. I asked her to tell me her story. Here's what she had to say:

"When I was twelve, I started reading *Seventeen* magazine and saw an article that said someone my height, five feet two inches, should weigh no more than 115 pounds. It took me years to realize that I had a large bone structure. There was no way that I could have weighed 115 in my lifetime unless I was anorexic. At the time, there wasn't the research that we now have regarding body mass index and what's healthy for your body type, so I believed the data in the article. I weighed 125 pounds, ten pounds more than the 'ideal' being presented in the magazine. To make matters worse, this was back when all of the kids in my class were lined up during gym and weighed. One teacher had you get on the scale and shouted out your weight to someone else who wrote it down. Every kid in my class now knew I weighed 125 pounds. It was horrifying and embarrassing all at once because now everyone else knew that I was ten pounds heavier than *Seventeen* said I should be too. I've never forgotten the impact that article had on my self-esteem and body image. From that moment on, I was in pursuit of seeing 115 on the scale. I wanted to be the 'ideal.' That single article gave me the perception that I was overweight. That perception lasted for more than forty years."

Whether we like it or not, we live in a world that puts an emphasis on how we look, more than on who we are—
surface over substance.

As long as you *look* fine, you *are* fine, right?

Nope, not necessarily.

What about the recent advertisement campaigns for Jenny Craig where actresses Kirstie Alley and Valerie Bertinelli were hired as spokeswomen for the company? Both had been beautiful bombshells at one time or another but had gained weight over the years. They made a public declaration that in order to be accepted, especially in Hollywood, they needed to improve their appearance. Kirstie Alley even starred in two semireality-based television shows called *Fat Actress* and *Big Life*, which focused on her lackluster career since she had gained weight and her struggles to lose it.

After she had lost her weight on Jenny Craig, Kirstie appeared on *Oprah* in a bikini. Unfortunately, she has gained back every pound she lost, and then some. Valerie wrote a best-selling book about her life and weight loss and touts her newfound love of life now that she is back to her old size. What kind of message is that? It reinforces the importance of looking good on the outside, but not the essential need to first feel good on the inside. Trust me, shedding pounds will not fix what's going on inside. **A *diet is a quick fix*,** and most of the time, the weight loss isn't permanent. The real work starts by working on what's wrong within.

> **FACT**
>
> A study found that 53 percent of thirteen-year-old American girls are unhappy with their bodies. By the time these girls are seventeen, that number will reach 78 percent.

Body image issues can start at almost any time but are often triggered by a certain moment, incident, or reaction we have to something that can make us feel inferior about ourselves. Let's all take a minute to think of when we first started or noticed our body image issues.

- ✔ **Did you come up with that moment?**
- ✔ **Did it suddenly change the way you thought about your size, shape, and weight?**
- ✔ **Did you begin comparing yourself to others?**

Research has shown that a change in body image can take place suddenly and often unexpectedly. As you get older, you may find you don't feel as good about yourself as you used to.

> *My father said I was so thin that my chest was inverted. Also, that if I turned sideways, all you'd see was my nose.* **—CYNTHIA, CHICAGO, ILLINOIS**

We all have that little voice inside our head telling us we're not good enough. It can tell us all sorts of negative stuff that makes us believe every word it's saying, whether it's true or not. That voice can talk you in or out of most anything, leading you to believe you are not talented, pretty, thin, or smart enough. But in reality, YOU ARE!

When you start thinking this way about yourself, I want you to ask yourself one very important question: Who else in your life would say those things about you? If your answer is nobody, then you know you are being too harsh on yourself. So stop!

When we are young, we are still in the process of developing our own thoughts and beliefs. Television, movies, magazines, and the Internet are all additional influences in developing how we see ourselves. Social networking sites, including Facebook, MySpace, and Twitter, put us out there in a very public way, and that can be debilitating if you're not secure with who you are.

Growing up, I wasn't allowed to watch violent or disturbing movies. *The Parent Trap* and *Grease* were about as risqué as things got in our home. Believe it or not, *Grease* was actually a push for my parents because of the hot-and-heavy make-out scenes. Numerous studies have shown that movies influence teens' behavior on everything, including drinking, smoking, and sex. According to the Centers for Disease Control, young people who see smoking or drinking in movies are more likely to smoke and drink too.

Teen People did a study showing that teens across the country continue to measure themselves against the people they see in movies, on television, and in magazines. According to the study, "of the 1,553 teenage girls surveyed, 58 percent said women on TV and in the movies, as well as the women portrayed in fashion magazines, cause them the most insecurity about their bodies."

It is almost impossible to avoid negative conditioning. I think our self-image is even more influenced by what those closest to us (our friends and family) say, think, and expect from us. If someone says you have chubby legs that jiggle, chances are you will see your legs the same way—and sadly, for some people, that perception can last for years if not a lifetime.

It never occurred to me that I might have big calves until I heard the older girls in the gym locker room looking at themselves and criticizing their bodies. Once I heard that, a seed was planted in me that took root and began to grow. I finally stopped hating myself when I learned to accept that I would never be a stick and that I could still have a good body and be curvy all at once. I actually like my curves now! I look in the mirror and appreciate my strong, curvy body. I like how my butt looks in jeans, and I love my height, even if in heels I tower over boys. This certainly wasn't always the case. It took a lot of time and effort to get to a place where I don't focus on my "flaws." I got here by realizing that standing in front of the mirror and picking out my flaws wouldn't get me anywhere. Especially focusing on things that I couldn't physically change.

You can stand in the mirror and nitpick all you want, but sooner or later you will be forced to find one good thing about your body. Once you do, your self-acceptance will blossom from there. If you can focus on accepting that one thing, your mind will be open to seeing other assets and will stop focusing only on the negative.

> **“** *I started to watch my body and criticize it when I entered high school and broke a hundred pounds. In high school, your weight was something discussed often with your girlfriends and you tended to say things like, 'I wish my butt wasn't so big, or my body shape was more like yours.'*
>
> **—LINDSEY M., BOULDER, COLORADO** **”**

> **“** *I first criticized my body around the age of nine or ten. The girls in my class would compare how much we weighed with each other, and my number was higher than some of the other girls'. I think that is when I began to have insecure feelings toward my body.*
>
> **—KATHRYN K., CINCINNATI, OHIO** **”**

> *In high school, it was hard to accept that I was the tall, willowy kid. The baby fat eventually went away and I turned thin. Growing up in Ohio, thin was not in fashion.*
>
> **—BETH, NEW YORK, NEW YORK**

The truth is that for most of us, we are the only ones who see those tiny flaws we spend hours staring at. Believe me, no one is staring at your big thighs like you think they are! Or if they are, it's likely they're admiring them!

I'm a Barbie Girl, in a *Barbie World.* . . .

Who among us didn't grow up playing with our Barbie dolls, pretending she was a real woman? An interesting fact is that for us girls, how we view our bodies can start when we are young, playing with our dolls. Believe it or not, these experiences can have a lasting impact. As I started to write this book, someone told me that my beloved Barbie doll was now a fifty-year-old icon. Yet she hadn't changed much from her earliest incarnation. She still had a tiny waist, impossibly long legs, a large chest, and long blond hair. In a way, she was the epitome of the women I saw every day in Los Angeles while I was growing up! I can't recall ever looking at my

Barbie and thinking, "She's so skinny," though I do remember thinking she was pretty. My sister, Christina, and I played with our Barbies because it was fun. Yet I was far more interested in all of her accessories than in her looks. I loved that she had her own house, car, salon, and really fashionable outfits. To me, Barbie was a strong, independent woman, but for most girls, she represents *the* **ideal** *woman.*

As funny as it might sound, there have actually been numerous studies done on the possibility of any real woman ever actually looking like a Barbie doll. A study conducted at the University of South Australia put the odds at one in 100,000, while the same group concluded that Barbie's other half, Ken's proportions, represented one out of every fifty men.

Does it seem a little strange to you that Ken's physique is so much more realistic than Barbie's? I guess I shouldn't be surprised. In perspective, society has always placed unrealistic expectations on women and their looks, so why wouldn't the makers of Barbie?

Many other studies have suggested that Barbie's proportions would be simply impossible to achieve by a real live woman. Researchers at Finland's University Central Hospital in Helsinki have gone as far as saying that "if Barbie were alive, she would lack the required 17 to 22 percent body fat required for a woman to have her period. So, impossible, no; but her measurements are certainly unhealthy and mostly unachievable."

All of this got me wondering about what impact Barbie, Bratz dolls, and all of the other toys we all grew up with actually have on young girls and their body image.

Is it possible that it was actually bad for us to have played with these "must have" toys when we were little? Or should we just look back on it as harmless fun?

Is the message these dolls send saying that we should starve ourselves to look undernourished, be stick thin with a perfect tan, always be dressed to the nines, and never be seen without makeup?

For some girls, *that early message cuts deep.*

When I was in elementary school, I had a girlfriend who came over to our house for a playdate. She and I went down to our playroom, and I pulled out all my Barbies and their fancy cars and dream houses. I was shocked and startled when I looked over and saw that my friend had ripped the head off one of my Barbies and then cut off all of her hair. At first I was so confused. Why would anyone want to hurt or ruin a beautiful Barbie? Further, I didn't understand why this little girl was so angry with my Barbie doll. It was only years later that I could comprehend that my friend was self-conscious about her own appearance, and Barbie represented something to her that she thought she could never measure up to. Her reaction was extreme but definitely not uncommon. In fact, I took a class at USC that touched on the effects Barbie has had on young girls. One study explored girls like my friend, who lash out at their Barbie dolls. Such girls often end up battling eating disorders as well as developing low self-esteem and other psychological concerns later in life.

One state lawmaker has gone so far as to try to pass a Barbie Ban Bill. Can you imagine? Jeff Eldridge, from Lincoln County, West Virginia, introduced a proposed ban on Barbie in his state because of the influence they have on young girls, which places too much importance on physical beauty at the expense of their intellectual and emotional development. While the bill didn't pass, I admire the thought behind it.

> *My uncle jokingly called me 'chunky butt.'*
> **—KIMBERLY M., ATLANTA, GEORGIA**

Girls of all ages and ethnicities are susceptible to having a negative body image, but for the most part, a woman's attitude about her body image is formed within her cultural environment and is the result of the various experiences she has had. Different cultures have different standards and norms for appropriate body size and shape. Some cultures celebrate a fuller body shape, while others think that a woman who is thin is the ideal woman.

FACT

A negative body image is most often seen among white, middle-class adolescent girls.

Maryanne Davidson from Yale University did a review of several research papers that found that "African American participants defined obesity in positive terms, relating it to attractiveness, sexual desirability, body image, strength or goodness, self-esteem and social acceptability. Interestingly, they didn't view obesity as a cause for concern when it came to their health." I love it that African American women embrace their curves. It seems more natural to *love the body you're given* than to constantly be in distress over it, right?

I can say from personal experience that where we grow up plays a big role in how positively we see ourselves and our bodies. I grew up in Los Angeles, and in Southern California looking perfect has become something of an art form. In Los Angeles, waking up in the morning and going to grab a coffee does not include walking casually out of the house in sweats and a baseball cap. In Beverly Hills, for example, every woman walking down the street has on a cute outfit, full makeup, hair perfectly done, and usually seems to be effortlessly walking around in three-inch heels. Most everyone is essentially and perpetually "ready for their close-up"! This was especially clear growing up as the daughter of celebrity parents. While my mom and dad never put pressure on my three siblings or me to look a certain way, they certainly encouraged all of us to be active, eat healthfully, and stay fit. Luckily for my sister and me, my mom was much more into natural beauty and always told us we were our most beautiful when we weren't wearing makeup.

The pressure in Los Angeles to appear as if you never age is also pervasive. It seems like no one dresses their age or acts their age anymore. My mother has refused to give in to the expectation that she should look like the majority of the women in Hollywood, and she has dodged the almost mandated plastic surgeon's scalpel.

Family, especially parents, plays a large role in the way girls grow up viewing their bodies, especially mothers and older sisters, who are essential role models in both positive and negative ways.

FACT

A 1991 Yale study showed that women who began dieting at an early age were more likely to have daughters who would engage in binge eating or have some type of eating disorder problem. These mothers were also more likely than other women to agree, when asked, that their daughters should lose weight.

> *My mother always spoke about her own weight and body image in an incredibly self-deprecating way when I was growing up. I constantly witnessed her saying negative things about her body. So, I became aware of my body image very early on—probably around third grade (age seven or eight).*
>
> **—KATHRYN K., CINCINNATI, OHIO**

My mother often tells a story about when she had her first ballet recital as a little girl. She was really excited about showing her family her dance performance, which she had worked hard on for weeks. When the time came for my mother to dance onstage, she knew she had totally rocked it, that is until she saw her mother backstage after her performance. She told my mother that she had done a wonderful job, except every time she leapt across the stage, the whole building shook. My mother was devastated by this remark, so much so that she never danced again and talks about and remembers that experience all of these years later.

When I was younger, I had no idea my sister, Christina, was paying close attention to my eating habits. Research shows that younger girls are impacted by their mothers, and I have no doubt they are also impacted by their sisters. She had to find her own way, as we all do, and today she is a beautiful nineteen-year-old and has taught me some healthy eating habits. My sister and I are very close today, thanks in part to those experiences we shared growing up. If you are lucky enough to have a sister around the same age as you, like I do, you should try to talk to each other about things, like how you are feeling about your body; after all, that's what sisters are there for.

Whether consciously or not, most parents teach their children there is great value and importance in being attractive. I have seen mothers who struggle to look like their teenage daughters and girls my age who want to look like they are older than their years. It's odd when I see mothers and daughters who can virtually pass for the same age.

Many parents make comments or suggestions to their kids that are hypercritical of their weight, appearance, and eating habits, thinking these statements are innocent and harmless without ever understanding that these remarks sting and often stick with us well beyond our teen years.

Comments such as

"Are you really going to eat that?"

and

"Maybe you shouldn't wear that"

really get under my skin because there are much nicer ways to get the point across. Whenever my mom or dad started down that path, I'd either leave the table in a huff or want to eat more. It's just better to keep your mouth shut about someone else's eating habits and focus on your own.

While most parents aren't deliberately trying to send a negative message to their daughter, they simply don't have a good sense that what they are saying, especially when combined with all of the other messages their daughter is exposed to every day, might leave an impression. For example, if a girl grows up overhearing her mother constantly complaining about her own weight, body, poor eating habits, and dieting, that is how that girl will be conditioned to think about herself. These comments not only contribute to but also actually reinforce that girl's negative self-image.

exercise

Make a list of all the negative comments you overhear for the next seven days. Write down every self-disparaging statement someone else says about themselves or that you make about yourself. When you've completed your list, ask yourself: *How does it make me feel?*

Were the majority of the comments about physical appearance?

Cross out all of those.

What are you left with?

What can you change about these statements to lessen the impact on your self-image?

Share your feelings with your family and friends so they know that what they say is hurting you and most likely them too.

Now, mothers, please pay

attention to this . . . it is my hope you will learn something valuable.

According to Dr. Christiane Northrup, moms need to own up to their own body image issues. Dr. Northrup told me about her experiences growing up watching her mother, who was not overweight but who frequently dieted, drank Metrecal, and was very conscious of her weight. While very little was ever said in her home about her mother's dieting habits, Dr. Northrup was greatly affected by what she saw, so much so that she didn't want to pass her mother's habits on to her own kids when they were teenagers. Despite her best efforts to protect her two daughters from dealing with their own body image issues, they had to go through it just like we all do. Moms, you can't stop your daughters from growing up. Part of that journey will include the development of their self-image. What you can do is try to create and provide a healthy environment for your daughters to grow up in. This is especially important when it comes to developing healthful habits about food and exercise. Doing this is the best gift that each mom can pass on to her daughter. Start by admitting to yourself and later maybe even to your daughter that you have your own body image issues and then deal with them. Your daughter's relationship to food and eating starts at home. So stop staring in the mirror and complaining about your wrinkles and how you have saggy skin and feel fat all the time. While you may think your daughters don't mind when you do that, they listen to it, and sooner or later they will be looking in the mirror and doing the same exact thing. You are now and forever will be the most important role model for your daughter.

If you think your daughter has any type of issue or concern about her body image or weight, first talk to her about it in a nice and nonjudgmental way. If that doesn't work, then talk to your pediatrician, who can bring up these issues at her next doctor's appointment. Let your family physician be the bad guy by explaining the health dangers of carrying excess weight or dieting at a young age. This type of information is received best by your child when it comes from an expert, such as her pediatrician or other physician. Parents giving their "opinions" or making "recommendations" to their teenagers can often backfire and lead to a daughter developing a hostile relationship toward food.

If you're not sure whether or not you may have body image issues, take a look at this list and notice the warning signs that may indicate you're struggling with a negative body image.

- ✔ You are extremely critical of yourself.
- ✔ You are extremely critical of your friends and others.
- ✔ You have an unrealistic definition of beauty.
- ✔ You are exercising more than usual or have become obsessive about hitting the gym.
- ✔ You have drastically changed your eating habits, including the amount of food, type of food, and how often you eat.
- ✔ You have a tremendous need to "fit in" and feel accepted by your peers and are willing to go to extremes to achieve that.
- ✔ You have low self-esteem.
- ✔ You feel ashamed and/or embarrassed by your appearance.
- ✔ You are self-conscious and worry about what other people think.
- ✔ You feel anxious and stressed-out all the time.
- ✔ You are unhappy and/or uncomfortable with your body.
- ✔ You feel sad or blue.
- ✔ You feel hopeless and unworthy.
- ✔ You pull back from your family, friends, and activities you used to enjoy.

If you notice that you said yes to some of these bullet points, no need to panic. It's just a good thing to be aware that you may have a negative body image, and perhaps now that you are aware of it you can be more conscious about correcting it.

FACT

According to a 2002 study by J. A. O'Dea, "poor self-esteem is associated with higher rates of withdrawal from friends and family, depression, suicide, smoking, alcohol and drug abuse."

If you are curious and want to know more about how you are feeling about your body image, answer the following questions. I created this short list to help you become aware of your own perceptions about yourself and others. And for all of you moms reading along, take a look at these questions and see how many apply to you too. Compare your answers to your daughter's; they may be a good indicator of how you both feel about your bodies. *Take a deep breath and proceed.*

BODY IMAGE
questionnaire

Do you avoid working out, hitting the gym, or going for a swim so no one can see your body?
Yes_____ No _____

Do you feel guilty or ashamed after every meal?
Yes_____ No _____

Are you consumed with the proportions of your body?
Yes_____ No _____

Are you concerned you will never fit the media's or society's image of the "perfect" body? Yes_____ No _____

Do you mainly wear black to look thinner?
Yes_____ No _____

Do you ever feel hatred, dissatisfaction, or awkward about your body? Yes_____ No _____

Is there a specific part of your body you would change?
Yes_____ No _____

Do you compare your body to others'? Yes_____ No _____

Are you dissatisfied with your body? Yes_____ No _____

If you answered yes to three or more questions, it is likely you have a negative body image.

Developing a positive body image at an early age is important because it will help you to feel good about yourself, even when times are confusing, overwhelming, and uncertain. If you're not busy dwelling on your looks, you'll have lots of time to put your energy into other things, such as developing stronger friendships, better relationships with your parents or siblings, doing better in school, and exploring outside interests such as sports, hobbies, or getting involved with volunteer work.

Riding horses was my refuge from whatever was going on in my life. The stable was a place where I could be free to be myself, have fun, and not think about school or teenage dramas. It gave me a safe place to clear my head and gather my thoughts. It is so important to be active, have lots of laughs, and do something you are passionate about and love every day. Since I didn't feel like I was ever really good in school, riding was a place where I could go and feel good about what I was doing.

I think it is essential for every girl, no matter her age, to clear her mind and do something she loves every day. When you excel in something—whether it's sports, art, music, acting, whatever you love to do—it helps build your self-esteem. So even if you're feeling a little down about how you look, being a good tennis player or singer or expert knitter will help people see you as special and make you feel special in return.

If you're an interesting, confident person, others will gravitate toward you!

Girls who feel good about themselves have an easier time making friends, take pride in their accomplishments, and are fairly upbeat most of the time. That positive attitude carries over into everything they do.

While there are some factors that will impact your body image that you simply can do nothing about, most of the other influences are within your control. You have a choice about how the opinions of others affect you.

Remember, it is common and completely normal to be a little bit if not totally interested in your appearance. We are women after all! I'm not telling you not to care about your appearance, just don't get overly obsessed. So if you obsess over what you're going to wear, feel awkward, shower three times a day, or feel like you will never measure up to others' standards for you, guess what?

You're not alone!

This is all common.

The good news is that most of you will work through your body image issues. The bad news is . . . it takes time, work, and practice. Hopefully, when you reach the end of this book, you will be on the way to a better you!

This section is for all you girls who are either going through teenage body changes or are about to experience them. These next few pages are filled with lots of helpful information I wish someone had told me when I was younger. If you've already been through these challenging times of change, you can skip this section and move ahead to the next on page 73.

CHAPTER 2

Let the *drama* Begin!

Dealing with *Body Changes*

> *I started growing breasts earlier than most girls in my class (fifth grade). A boy on the bus made a comment that my sports bra, which was more like a fitted tank top, was sticking out of my shirtsleeve. I was mortified. I did not like 'developing' early.*
>
> **—KATHRYN K., CINCINNATI, OHIO**

Were you one of those girls who woke up one morning, looked in the mirror, and suddenly noticed that you were getting taller and bigger . . . in all directions? Maybe you noticed a little rounder rear, like suddenly "baby got back," or a rapid swelling—or as my friends called mine, swollen bug bites or bee stings—in your chest that wasn't there the night before? Perhaps you woke up crying or upset for no apparent reason and without any logical explanation?

Uh-huh.

It's happening.

Right before your very eyes.

You are officially becoming a woman!

Don't panic.
Get excited!

No one really prepared me for what was about to set in when I became a woman. I was aware that changes were taking place in my body, and I hated every minute of it. I was in the fourth grade when we had to sit through the lame sex ed class in school. The teacher put on a movie for us to watch that made it clear that yes, eventually, my breasts would grow, my hips would get bigger, I would get my period, and I might begin to develop "feelings" for boys. I heard the information, but truthfully, none of it really registered. None of these changes were at the forefront of my mind because as it turned out, I developed much later than my friends did. I was in the ninth grade by the time my body began to visibly change.

I am not sure if horseback riding all the time had anything to do with my late development, but it certainly brings up one of my most vivid memories of the first time someone made a comment about my new body.

I had gone away for a few weeks with my family and hadn't been to the barn for some time. When I came back to ride, the mother of one of the other riders stopped me and said, "Wow! You've got a big butt and you finally have hips! You've really changed since the last time I saw you!"

"Oh . . . No . . . She . . . Didn't!" I thought to myself.

I was horrified by her words.

Riding clothes are really tight fitting. I hadn't noticed the changes, but apparently they were obvious that particular day in the stall as I was putting away my horse.

I was so embarrassed by the comments my friend's mother made that I didn't want to repeat them to anyone. Girls are so emotional at this stage in life as it is. I didn't want to hear that I had a big butt and hips, *especially* from someone else's mother. While I believe she meant what she was saying as a compliment, her words hurt, and I've never forgotten them. She should have been more thoughtful in her choice of words, saying, "You look beautiful." But she didn't. As far as I was concerned, that comment was the beginning of the end.

I didn't really understand that my body was in transition. I had no clue that what was taking place inside my body was now also showing on the outside. All I knew was that my riding clothes still fit, so it never occurred to me that I was gaining weight. And as if it wasn't already obvious enough, my new bodacious body became painfully clear after my little brother commented on my new shape.

We were standing on the stairs in our home. I was wearing tight stretch pants. They were just comfortable clothes that weren't meant to be a fashion statement. When I am home, I don't really care about looking perfect all the time, especially when I am just lounging. I noticed my brother was staring at my body and not listening to whatever I was saying.

"Wow, you're really filling out!" he said.

Ouch.

"Thanks for sharing" was the best comeback I could swing before running up the stairs to my room, slamming the door, and refusing to come out for the rest of the evening. While I know my brother didn't mean that in a hurtful way, it was pretty unnecessary for him to state the obvious.

Girls, make a note of this: boys, especially brothers, will make comments about your development.

We develop and become more mature at a faster rate than they do. They observe our changes and for some reason find it important to let us know we're getting boobs or we have a zit on our face. **WE ALL KNOW IT!** We looked in the mirror that morning and saw it too! No need to say anything to our faces about it!

It was weird to suddenly hear these comments because I had never had a round rear end. It was always pretty flat. And then, without warning, I started getting curvier, which everyone noticed . . . except me! Suddenly my body wasn't straight up and down anymore like a boy's. I had a round butt and hips. I was developing feminine characteristics. A woman's body is supposed to be curvy. Curves don't make you fat—they make you feminine. But it didn't feel like that at the time. No way. All I felt was fat and blobby!

This can be a confusing and overwhelming time because your body is going through so many changes at once. Most girls think that getting a period is the first sign that your body is changing, but that's not necessarily so. In fact, your body starts changing in all sorts of ways long before menstruation begins.

Although I had seen the movie in my sex ed class back in the fourth grade, and yes, my mom explained the basics about my "coming of age" and "becoming a woman," I never had a great understanding of what really goes on in our bodies as we mature and change. So I thought I'd compile a list just for you girls of the possible and likely changes you might notice as your body is changing. It may seem totally overwhelming at first, but don't worry. It doesn't happen all at once! Just relax!

- O Your height and weight will increase.
- O Your hips will get wider.
- O Your body will become curvier.
- O Your boobs will get bigger.
- O You will get hair down there.
- O You will get hair under your arms.
- O You will get your period.
- O Your hair and skin may become noticeably oily.
- O You may get acne.
- O You will sweat more.
- O You will be hungrier.
- O You will have increased hormone levels, which might make you more irritable.

Now, I know that most of you just read that list and thought, "Great, becoming a woman sucks." But think again. While it is weird at first to have all of these changes happen to you, you will eventually learn to embrace them and accept them and, most of all, love them.

Your *Hips* Don't Lie

While I knew my hips would get wider as part of my body's changes, no one ever explained to me why this happens, so I thought I'd share the reason with you so you can understand it's not just some cruel joke. Our hips widen for a reason.

The pelvis widens to allow you to have a baby. That's the only reason the hips shift. Any added padding is a function of your eating or lack of physical activity.

Finally, as you change, what you perceive as getting fat is a normal part of transitioning from being a girl to being a woman. Most women carry a large percentage of body fat in their breasts, hips, booty, thighs, and upper arms. There are several factors that contribute to our overall body shape, including genetics, environment, how fat gets distributed throughout our body, and growth.

Sad, but *True* . . .

According to Dr. Marie Savard, "At age ten, the average girl has 6 percent more body fat than the average boy, but by the end of puberty, the difference is nearly 50 percent higher for girls." Guys have it so easy, don't they!

With all of these changes taking place, it's no wonder you may feel confused or uncertain about what's happening inside and outside your body. It's a difficult time for everyone. There's no right or wrong way to go through these changes. Like the Nike ad says, you've got to "just do it."

You can't prevent these changes from happening, so you may as well prepare yourself to be as ready for them as possible. There were plenty of days I freaked out over my body changing. But I've learned to love my body. It's strong and healthy. We have to treat our bodies with care because we only get one!

No *Ifs*, *Ands*, or *Buts* . . . It's Your Period!

Aunt Flow has arrived . . . or IT . . . as in, I Got IT. . . . Whatever you call it, your period is here to stay.

A lot of girls consider the onset of their period to be the end of puberty. Well, sorry to be the bearer of bad news, but having your period doesn't mean you're done—you're really just starting to change. Everyone has an embarrassing story about their first period. But I promise that you will survive yours and even laugh about it someday!

While most of my friends got their periods in the seventh and eighth grades, I didn't get mine until the beginning of ninth grade. I got it at the worst time possible! I was on a weekend school retreat in the woods with all of my classmates. I knew I was the only one of my friends who still hadn't gotten her period, but I certainly wasn't expecting it that weekend. As we were all boarding the bus to leave for Catalina Island, I noticed a strange feeling— like I had to go to the bathroom, but different. I walked to the back of the bus, opened the tiny door to the bathroom, and . . . there it was.

"You've got to be kidding me!" I said aloud, even though no one could hear me.

I didn't want to tell any of my friends what had happened. I knew they would make a big deal out of it, since I was the last one in our group of friends to get my period. So I stuffed a bunch of Kleenex inside my underwear and hoped it would just stop. But, of course, it didn't.

I called my mom on her cell phone just as we were pulling out of the parking lot to tell her what had happened. She wasn't emotional about the onset of my menstrual cycle like some other mothers I knew, who cried and got upset when their daughters got theirs. My mom was very matter-of-fact and calm, as if it was just another normal day. I suppose that was a smart decision on her part because I was on my way for a weekend in the wilderness, whether I had my period or not.

On the boat ride to the island, I finally told a couple of my friends what had happened, mostly because I didn't have a tampon with me and I was afraid I might leak through my jeans. And even if I did have a tampon, I certainly had no idea how to use one. I couldn't have been less prepared for this moment. Thankfully, one of the girls had a pad with her. I went back to the bathroom with the pad carefully hidden beneath my shirt. I pulled off the protective strips and placed it inside my underwear. It felt like I was wearing an adult diaper under my jeans. So uncomfortable!

Could this story get any worse?

I'm afraid so.

You see, the week before we went on this retreat I had just gotten my first boyfriend, who unfortunately was on the trip with us too. I kept running away from him every time he tried to talk to me. It was awful. I was so embarrassed and worried he would know what was up, which, a few hours later, led to our breakup. That relationship endured for two whole days. It was a fond memory while it lasted.

Our first activity after we arrived was . . . you guessed it, *swimming*. I didn't want to tell my male teacher I couldn't go in the water. That was the most horrifying thought, so I put another pad inside the bottom half of my bikini bathing suit and jumped in the water, praying that no one would notice the giant bulge, or worse, that it might somehow come loose and float up in the water. Thankfully, it stayed in place and I was able to figure out a discreet way to change my pad every thirty minutes for the rest of the weekend without anyone being the wiser.

I didn't learn how to use a tampon until a year or so after I began my first period. I found them to be so confusing. I had no idea where it was supposed to go. I knew it should be inserted somewhere "down there," but I couldn't seem to grasp exactly "where." All tampon manufacturers offer directions that come with a box of these tubes filled with absorbent cottonlike material. If, however, you find the directions to be a little like putting together a piece of furniture from IKEA, then you're not alone. My mother tried to show me the right way to use a tampon, but it totally grossed me out. Then a few of my girlfriends were shocked that I was still using pads, so they too tried to teach me. I can remember one of my friends sat in the bathroom with me for nearly two hours, coaching me as I tried one tampon after another until I finally gave up out of pure frustration and confusion! The first time I successfully used a tampon was after my mother's gynecologist showed me how. Once I realized it wasn't that big a deal, I was able to get over my phobia and have been using them ever since.

My first period lasted three days. I was so happy when it was over—that is, until I realized my period would return for another torturous few days month after month.

Does the thought of getting your period freak you out?

Having your first period is the most dramatic, if not traumatic, sign that your body is really, and I mean really, about to change.

While *getting* mine didn't actually bother me, the circumstances were not the most ideal. I would have preferred to have been at home, able to shower and deal with this next milestone in the privacy of my own bathroom. But nature has a funny way of taking its course. There's no way to predict when you will get your period, but most girls will begin to menstruate somewhere between the ages of nine and fifteen. A good indicator is within two years after you begin to develop breasts. Your mom or older sisters can also give you some insight, as heredity plays a role in when you will get yours. If they started menstruating later or earlier, chances are you will too.

The best advice I can offer you is to be prepared and don't freak out. ***Know what to expect, even when it's unexpected.***

To get you through, here's what you need to know about all of the possible side effects.

✔ Period cramps are actually contractions of the uterus. They're very real and, for some girls, very painful. If you have severe cramping during your period, tell your mom or contact your doctor, as this can sometimes be the sign of something more serious than plain old cramps.

✔ Exercise is one of the best ways to beat your cramps, and it helps you feel less bloated too. If the thought of jumping around is more than you can bear, try taking a warm bath or using a heating pad on your pelvic area to alleviate your discomfort.

✔ Days before you're about to start your period, you may notice your breasts getting sore. This is caused by hormones in your bloodstream that can make certain parts of your body extrasensitive. Your breasts are especially prone to this discomfort. Breathe a sigh of relief to know the pain is temporary. A day or two in, and you'll begin to notice they're not as sore, and by the time you're done with your period, they ought to be back to normal.

✔ If your breasts do get sore, avoid wearing for those few days any tight-fitting clothes that might restrict your breasts. If you're already wearing a bra, try to avoid wearing one that has an underwire or coarse material such as stiff lace. If you want to be especially comfortable, you can substitute a sports bra, camisole, or tank top for your regular bra during those couple of days.

✔ PMS, or premenstrual syndrome, is caused by hormone fluctuations throughout your cycle. These changes can impact your energy level, emotions, and body by causing aches and pains in your lower back, breasts, and pelvic area. You may even begin to feel grouchy, inexplicably sad, or downright depressed. These are all normal symptoms that can be just a nuisance or become debilitating if you let them get out of hand. Instead of snapping at your mom, sister, or best friend, take a deep breath and realize that this too shall pass. One helpful hint I've found is to limit the amount of sugar you eat in the days before your period, which will help stabilize your mood. Also, diet and exercise are the best defenses when it comes to how you feel. Some experts recommend taking vitamin B_6, evening primrose oil, or calcium or magnesium supplements to help the symptoms of PMS subside. Talk to your family doctor before taking any medications, even supplements, to make sure they're right for your needs.

Make sure you try to stay active and eat right, even when you feel like crawling under the covers and hiding from the world until the worst is behind you.

I was now a woman, which sounds romantic and mushy, but I was feeling angst and animosity about it. I reluctantly let go of my resistance and began to embrace the experience.

After all, what choice did I have? The train had definitely left the station, and I wasn't getting off it anytime soon. Next stop . . . breasts and butt!

SECRET . . . ACCIDENTS HAPPEN.

2 If you haven't already gotten your period, I assure you that every girl who has lived before you has bled through her pants, skirt, or dress at one time or another. It's embarrassing when it happens, but it does happen. My first piece of advice to you is to stay calm.

DO NOT PANIC!

Although I am certain you'll want to run out of the room from utter embarrassment, you'll just call more attention to yourself if you do. There's no way to ignore the obvious, but I have a great secret tip. If you've got your period, keep a long sweater, jacket, or sweatshirt tied around your shoulders or in your locker at school. If you do have an unexpected leak, you can tie that piece of extra clothing around your waist and hide the evidence until you can get someplace safe to change into something new.

Remember, when it comes to all of the changes you're going through during these years, your mom went through them too when she was your age. If you have questions about what's happening, talk with her. You may be surprised to find out that she felt exactly the same way you do. Plus, it will inevitably bring you closer as mother and daughter.

There are normal and predictable times in life when a girl's body image can become naturally distorted. All of a sudden you become very aware of your body, how it looks, and worse, how *you* think it looks! I call this reality vs. perception. This new way of seeing yourself in the mirror will be scary at first, but **don't worry,** everyone goes through it. As girls' bodies change, they tend to gain fat in their breasts, hips, butt, and thighs, developing a more shapely body than they had as an adolescent. You might not like your curvy butt or big boobs now, but trust me, you will. It's just a matter of time.

You may view your body as being heavier than it actually is, especially when you start to compare yourself to other girls, fashion models, or celebrities. It may seem like a good idea to compare yourself to these other girls, but it's important to remember that every *body* is different. If your body doesn't look like theirs, there's nothing wrong with you. It just means you're unique—we all are, and that's what makes each of us special.

I want to encourage you to love your body no matter what your size, though I realize there are body issues that can mortify, humiliate, confuse, and cause DRAMA. There isn't one type of "normal," but I want to offer reassurance and a reality check about some of these body dilemmas.

Whether you want to admit it or not, studies show that more than 50 percent of girls in high school admit to being sexually active, including having intercourse. The reality is that the number could be higher, but not all girls will admit their activity. In fact, girls today, especially because of the Internet and TV shows, know as much about sex at age ten or eleven as I did at age sixteen! That is why I have included this section in the book. It is my humble opinion that your daughter probably knows more than you think she does. Many of my younger girl cousins have asked me about sex, birth control, and what to expect. My brother approached my mother to explain what an STD was after seeing it on the cover of a magazine . . . and he was only twelve!

About a week or two after I got my first period, I had a sudden realization that I could now get pregnant. Even though I wasn't sexually active at that point, I thought it made sense to talk to someone about birth control so I could understand all of my options when the time was right.

Since both of my parents were busy working, we had a nanny to help take care of me and my brothers and sister. She was more like an older sister than a nanny. I usually talked to her first about personal stuff I wasn't quite ready to go to my parents with—and birth control was one of those conversations. She told me that going on the pill can have certain side effects, such as water retention and weight gain.

The only other thing I had heard about going on birth control pills was that they made your breasts get really big. I thought, "What's wrong with that?" After all, I was flat chested my whole life. I was excited about finally getting breasts!

"Bring it on!" I thought.

What no one told me was that the pill can also make you feel like you're wearing a fat suit. You may gain weight, and not just in your breasts—you may gain it all over. I didn't realize that was a potential side effect when I decided to finally go on the pill in the tenth grade. The only thing I was aware of was waking up in the morning feeling constantly bloated. I'd go to spin class five days a week but never lost that thick feeling. I worked out, ate right, but couldn't drop those newly added pounds after going on the pill. It was awful, so I decided to find an alternative plan to practice safe and effective birth control. And when I did, I lost the excess water weight I put on from being on the pill. This doesn't happen to everyone, because everyone's body is different. But be aware of side effects when you're thinking about going on the pill. And *if you're having sex, ALWAYS use some form of birth control.* It's up to you, not your partner (though if he's a stand-up guy he will respect your decision and take the initiative), to take care of your body and practice safe sex.

I remember hearing about my first friend who finally did go on the pill, and it seemed like such a big deal. A lot of the girls I knew first went on the pill to regulate their periods, but there were a few who started taking it because they were having sex. I never had any friends who got pregnant in high school because there was so much awareness about birth control, but there were plenty of scares. One friend was so overdramatic that every time she slept with her boyfriend she thought she was pregnant. If her period was a day late, she would call me sobbing, convinced she was preggers.

FACT

Research has shown that teenagers who can talk openly with their parents about sex are more likely to resist peer pressure to have intercourse and will postpone their first time. They are also more likely to be responsible, choosing to practice safe sex, when they do become active.

"You're not pregnant," I'd try to say reassuringly. "You just have a food baby!" referring to her nervous eating habit. I would take her to the local pharmacy to buy a home pregnancy kit. She'd dutifully pee on the stick, but it always came back negative.

To be certain, high school is all about drama. Baby drama shouldn't be something you knowingly want to deal with—especially in high school and college—so here's what you need to know to keep that issue at bay.

Talk to your daughter about birth control when you feel the time is right. The sooner the better, because believe me, it is out there. It is far better for your daughter to hear the truth from you, her mother, than to get caught up in the myths.

FACT

While abstinence is by far the safest choice when it comes to avoiding pregnancy or the spread of disease, it's not terribly realistic to think kids won't be tempted to explore their sexuality at some point in their teen years. A recent study done by John B. Jemmott III, PhD, professor of communication in psychiatry and of communications at the University of Pennsylvania, states, "The younger someone is when they have sex for the first time, the less likely they are to use condoms."

It's important to know your options and responsibilities when it comes to sex. You have to be properly informed to make decisions about your body, including honoring your desires, values, and beliefs. If you don't want to be sexually active, you have the right to say no. No guy has the right to tell you what's right for you. Don't let anyone talk you into doing something you're not ready for.

I saw an episode of *Oprah* a few years ago about a fourteen-year-old couple who agreed to be on the show to talk about losing their virginity and having sex for the very first time. They appeared with both sets of parents, who were trying to talk them out of it. Well-known sex therapist Dr. Laura Berman explained to the young girl that boys have a much different perspective when it comes to longevity in relationships. To prove her point, she asked the girl how long she thought she would be with her boyfriend. Her answer took the duo through high school and college together. When Dr. Berman asked the boy the same question, he answered, "Six months."

The reaction from the audience was audible. The girl never let go of her boyfriend's hand throughout the interview, but she quickly changed her mind about deciding to sleep with him.

If you're not emotionally ready for a sexual relationship, it's okay. Be strong and stand your ground when it comes to saying no. Many girls believe they don't have the power and strength to say no and then give in to pressure from their boyfriends. They wind up having sex anyway and then feel awful about it after. Most girls think that having sex will bring them closer to their boyfriends and make their relationships stronger, but this is rarely the case. Boys, especially in high school, mostly want to be sexual for the idea of having sex and then bragging about it to their friends, while girls want to have sex to "make love" and be closer to their boyfriend. *It's far more emotional for the girl,* and mostly just physical for the boy.

When a boy says he won't talk about your sexual escapades, he's lying. When he says he won't spill the juicy details about it to everyone, he's also lying. Boys talk more than girls, especially when it comes to sexual conquests. If you don't feel like you want to have sex and are uncomfortable doing it, then stand your ground and don't go through with it until you are absolutely certain it is what *you* want. Sexual exploration is very normal during your teens and twenties. But make sure you act responsibly, which means using a contraceptive—a medication or device that prevents pregnancy and the spread of STDs.

FACT

According to a 2009 University of Pittsburgh study, overweight Caucasian girls are less likely to use condoms when having intercourse than thinner girls. The same study reported that underweight African American girls were also less likely to use condoms, while Latina girls of all weights were more likely to engage in sexual activity without using a condom or oral contraception.

Birth Control *Options*

Women have been practicing birth control for centuries. Research has uncovered instructions dating back to 1500 B.C. that describe how to prepare an herbal contraceptive. That's a long time!

More modern methods of birth control include:

✔ *Condoms,* a tight-fitting latex or polyurethane covering for the penis. Condoms are the safest form of birth control to use when you also want to avoid the possibility of contracting a sexually transmitted disease (STD). It's important to know that though using a condom is safe, they're not completely foolproof. If they tear, slip off, or break during intercourse, you risk pregnancy or being exposed to an STD.

✔ STDs are why *spermicides,* a cream, gel, or foam, are often used for extra protection inside the vagina or around a condom, although it is important to know these won't work on their own. They must be used in combination with some other form of birth control.

✔ *Birth control pills* come in either a progesterone-only pill, which is 98 percent effective when taken exactly as prescribed (95 percent when taken typically by most users, who may miss a pill or take it later or earlier on a particular day), or a combined pill, which is 99 percent effective when taken exactly as prescribed, making it the most effective against pregnancy when used perfectly. If it isn't taken exactly as prescribed, it too is only 95 percent effective. This pill works by stopping your eggs from maturing so you won't release any eggs when you ovulate. Birth control pills must be taken exactly as prescribed to work right. Any deviation reduces their reliability and increases your risk for pregnancy.

✔ *Birth control patches* work similarly to the pill, except you don't need to take them orally. The hormones are released through the adhesive patch you wear.

While most girls have no side effects from taking an oral contraceptive, it is possible that you could feel the impact when you first start.

Common side effects include:

✔ some light spotting in the beginning
✔ nausea
✔ headaches
✔ mood changes
✔ sore or enlarged breasts
✔ high blood pressure
✔ weight gain

There are no calories in the pill, but you may find that taking it makes you hungrier than usual, so it's important to watch your portion sizes, avoid eating junk food, and drink lots of water! We all get that bloated feeling when we have our periods anyway. Water will help flush that excess bloat out of your body, leaving you feeling better in no time.

But taking the pill can also have some positive medical benefits. It can:

✔ regulate your menstrual cycle
✔ help prevent painful periods
✔ reduce or eliminate cramps
✔ lighten a heavy flow
✔ improve or clear up your mild acne

The hormones in the pill can stop acne from forming, but it takes time to see the results of this benefit, sometimes as long as two to three months. One other medical benefit from taking the pill is that it decreases your chances of developing endometrial cancer, ovarian cancer, and ovarian cysts.

If you are considering birth control, you need to talk to your doctor about which method is right for you. He or she can take all of your personal factors into account, including your weight, to help you select the right birth control for your needs, and to help minimize the weight gain or other side effects that are common to starting the pill or patch.

Here's the most important thing to know about contraceptives—*they only work when they're used, and they must be used properly every time to avoid the risk of pregnancy.*

Acne

Just when you thought things couldn't get any worse, along comes your first gigantic zit!

We've all been there or will go there, so you may as well know the "dos" and "don'ts" of acne. Your face is oftentimes the first thing people notice, which is why it is so important to take care of it.

FACT:

TRUE OR FALSE?

Eating chocolate can cause acne.
. . . **FALSE!**

Despite folklore to the contrary, chocolate does not cause acne. Neither do greasy or fried foods. Eating oily foods does not affect the skin's degree of oiliness.

Pimples are blemishes that appear when the skin produces an oily substance called sebum that clogs your hair follicles under your skin. This blockage causes either a blackhead or a whitehead. If bacteria get trapped in the follicle and grow, it can cause a reaction that makes that blemish look inflamed, enlarged, ready to erupt like

Mount St. Helens! The gross stuff inside that infected blemish is pus, which is produced when your body is trying to fight off the bacteria that are trapped inside the follicle. DON'T TOUCH IT! This is what doctors refer to as acne.

To understand what causes acne, let's take a quick look at your facial skin and why it is so important.

Skin is a great mirror to your health. It can reflect good health or it can show signs that something is wrong or missing from your diet. Think of it as an outside marker of what's happening on your inside. Not eating a healthful and balanced diet may first be reflected in your skin's appearance.

Did you know that your skin is the largest organ of your body? Something interfering with your body might show up on the outside of your skin. Think about it. According to Park Avenue dermatologist and founder of DermTV, Dr. Neal Schultz, "Each square inch of your skin contains blood vessels, sweat glands, and nerve endings that measure your body temperature, pain, touch, and pressure. Through nerve impulses transmitted to the brain, the skin protects the body from injury."

The skin has many vital protective functions; it protects the underlying tissues from invasion by bacteria, from the sun's harmful rays, and from the toxic substances in the environment we are all exposed to both inside and outside our homes every single day. In addition to keeping undesirable things out, skin keeps in moisture and the chemicals we need to be healthy.

Although most of us worry about breakouts on our face, acne can develop and appear all over your body, including your neck, chest, back, booty, arms, and thighs. It's a lot easier to hide pimples that appear in those less obvious locations, but it doesn't make it any more comfortable.

Since we are all different, some girls will be more prone to breaking out than others. It may not seem fair that your best friends all have perfect skin while yours is beginning to look like a "connect-the-dots" game. It all depends on how your body reacts to the hormones that are now running rampant through your system. Acne tends to be hereditary, so if your mom, dad, or siblings struggled with it when they were younger, chances are you will too.

Like all of our organs, our skin, hair, and nails receive their nutrition from the nutrients absorbed into the bloodstream from the foods we eat. Believe it or not, the skin receives up to one-third of the blood circulating in the body! The food we eat is one of the most important elements to having vibrant, clear, and healthy-looking skin. It's important to eat the right types of food, which give your skin the proper vitamins and minerals, including iron and vitamins A, B, C, and D, as well as essential amino acids— all of the elements it takes to run the metabolic machine of the human body. Your body can't create these vitamins—

you have to eat them or take some type of supplement. The important thing is to understand what foods you should include in your daily diet to be certain you are getting all of the essential vitamins and minerals to help keep your skin looking and feeling great. *(More on that in chapter 6.)*

It may seem a little strange to read about nutrition when I am talking about the importance of our skin, but as an old saying goes, ***"We are what we eat."*** And if that is true, our skin is the reflection, the mirror from your inside to what the rest of us see on the outside.

While the foods you eat won't prevent acne when you are a teen or even an adult, they can certainly have a positive impact on the luster, clarity, and overall appearance of your skin. Your facial skin is your calling card to the world. If you find yourself dealing with chronic acne, you may want to consider changing up your diet to help improve your facial skin.

SECRET . . . THE FRIED FOOD MYTH.

3

Greasy, oily, or fried food will not give you acne! The only thing that can increase the activity of oil glands is male hormones.

What can you do to help prevent breakouts or stop them from getting worse once they happen?

1. Don't stress! If you're prone to acne or breakouts
when you're stressed about a test, relationship, or some other drama, it's because your adrenal glands are being stimulated, which increases your oil gland production. Your pores can become blocked because dead skin cells won't flake off like they normally do. This blockage is what triggers the bacteria in our skin to multiply, which can lead to a breakout. Get rid of whatever is stressing you out! Nothing good comes from it!

2. Don't pick! As tempted as we all are when it comes to
zits, the gross truth is they're filled with bacteria. Picking, popping, poking, pushing, or squeezing these unsightly pimples cause the infection to spread. And if you're not careful, you can actually cause damage to the skin that can result in scars, pockmarks, and scabs. A couple of days being left alone is a lot better than a lifetime reminder that your mother was right when she said "Don't pick!" Dr. Schultz actually tells his patients to call him for a free visit, which he refers to as his "emergency pimple policy," to help his patients refrain from causing more damage to their skin. A family friend who is also a licensed aesthetician has the same policy. Whenever I feel a pimple coming on, I will drive right over to her shop so she can deal with it the right

way. Bottom line: just don't touch it! Leave it be and it will go away, or if you have one, make a quick appointment with your dermatologist!

3. *Hair and makeup.* If you are prone to pimples, try to wear less makeup during a breakout, and only use products that are oil-free or non-comedogenic, which means they won't clog your pores. Some girls may notice breakouts around their hairline. If this happens to you, try a different shampoo to see if that helps clear up the acne around your forehead. Also, if you work out wearing a baseball hat, you may be irritating your skin where the sweat and your hat meet. Try removing your hat for a few days to see if that helps clear things up too.

Trying to cover up a pimple is sometimes worse than just letting it be. If you don't have the right makeup or skill, you can actually make it look worse. Let the blemish run its course. If you do, you'll find that in a few short days, it will quickly disappear.

SECRET . . . GO NAKED.

4. One day a week, go without makeup in public, and celebrate your true beauty.

Skin, Genetics, and the Sun

As long as we're on the topic of skin care, a lot of girls worry that if their mom has lots of wrinkles, sun damage, and skin discoloration, they will grow up with the same conditions. Genetics will tell the tale for many features, such as your eyes, hair, shape of your nose, and even body shape, but they aren't a major factor in your skin. Your lifestyle will determine how you age. If you're a sun worshiper, chances are you will regret that Hawaiian tan when you get older. Even tanning beds and spray tans can damage your skin, so my advice is to avoid any extended exposure if you aren't wearing sunscreen.

FACT
The average woman has 20,000 pores!

There's a lot you can do to protect your skin now so you don't pay the price later.

1. Start wearing sunscreen every day!

Sunscreen protects you from the sun's damaging rays, which can cause sunburn, wrinkles, freckling, premature aging, and, of course, skin cancer. Broad-spectrum sunscreens are oil-free and non-comedogenic, meaning they won't block your pores. So go ahead and have fun in the sun—you're protected! Even if it's cloudy out, protect your skin against the sun's harmful ultraviolet rays by generously applying sunscreen before you put on your makeup. And just in case you didn't know this, most makeup doesn't offer any protection from the sun unless it contains an SPF, sun protection factor, or an EPF, environmental protection factor, so wearing more makeup isn't an alternative to wearing sunscreen. Recent studies show that 20 percent of sun damage is done before we turn eighteen years old. It's never too late to start protecting your skin. For the best protection make sure you use a sunscreen with an SPF of at least 30 or higher.

2. *Eat a healthful diet!* Choose foods that aren't high in fat, are natural, and contain fewer preservatives. (See chapter 6 for some helpful hints on foods that will benefit you and your skin.)

3. *Avoid smoking.* It's true that smokers develop smoker's lines around their lips. Those never go away, at least not without expensive fillers. Plus, smoking is just gross. If you've ever been around someone who smokes, you know they always smell like smoke, usually have stinky breath, and are flirting with being one step closer to cancer every time they light up.

4. Avoid overindulging in alcohol.

Excessive alcohol consumption can have all sorts of negative effects on you, including bloating and weight gain, and can lead to liver disease and even cause rosacea, a condition that causes redness of the nose! If you don't want to turn into Rudolph the Red-Nosed Reindeer, drink moderately! Your head and body will thank you for it later.

Seven facts about media exposure we should all know

1. *The average U.S. resident is exposed to approximately 5,000 advertising messages a day.*

2. *According to a recent survey of adolescent girls, their main source of information about women's health issues comes from the media.*

3. *Researchers estimate that 60 percent of Caucasian middle-school girls regularly read at least one fashion magazine.*

4. *Another study of mass media magazines discovered that women's magazines had ten times more advertisements and articles promoting weight loss than men's magazines.*

5. *The average adolescent watches three to four hours of television a day.*

6. *A study of 4,294 network television commercials revealed that 1 out of every 3.8 commercials sends some sort of "attractiveness message" telling viewers what is or is not attractive.*

7. *The average adolescent sees over 5,260 attractiveness messages a year.*

CHAPTER 3

Overexposure

how the *media* influence our *body* image

> " *I really appreciate seeing a healthy-looking woman in the media. Sadly, it's a rare sighting these days. I actually think many celebrities look sickly thin and all of the 'work' they've had done is, for the most part, unflattering. I think about my weight constantly and I can't remember a time when I felt like I didn't need to lose fifteen pounds. I wish I didn't.*
>
> —RACHEL, NEW YORK, NEW YORK "

93

> *I think celebrities all look so similar that it becomes 'normal' to us in the real world. Then, once you get back to the real world, you realize it's not all Hollywood bodies. To an extent, you always know in the back of your mind that what you're seeing on television and in magazines is not really the way the person looks.*
>
> **—AUDREY, ZANESVILLE, OHIO**

"Look like this and be sexy."
"THIN IS IN."
"LOSE TEN POUNDS IN THREE DAYS!"
"Here's what you need to fix. . . ."

These are the messages most of us are being blasted with daily.

About halfway through my last semester of high school, I began to notice these amazing ads in magazines for Dove soap. The campaign focused on using real women—not models—of all shapes and sizes to represent all types of natural and real beauty. The women were photographed wearing nothing but their underwear and bras and a big happy smile. I remember the first time I saw a giant billboard for Dove in the middle of Hollywood—a city obsessed with beauty where full lips, big boobs, tiny waists, and long, luscious hair extensions and surgical enhancements are all the rage—I stopped in my tracks. The juxtaposition of Dove's idea of beauty set against the Hollywood glitz and glamour was intriguing, if not a little bit ironic. The ad never made it clear it was promoting soap or any other product, which I loved. None of the women were holding a bar of soap. The billboard simply read DOVE at the bottom of the photo.

I had already been accepted to and was ready to start my freshman year of college at the University of Southern California in the fall of 2008, where I planned to major in communications with a minor in gender studies. I was so intrigued by the Dove campaign because it touched on both my major and minor, and to be honest, brought to the surface insecurities I'd been battling for years. As a way to get a jump start on my college studies, I began researching what their campaign was all about. I wanted to know why they were using women in their underwear to promote their product and not typical skinny supermodel types. That's when I came across their Web site promoting "Real Beauty."

The Web site described the Dove campaign for Real Beauty as "a worldwide marketing strategy to celebrate the natural physical variation embodied by all women and inspire them to have the confidence to be comfortable with themselves." The focus was to promote real, natural beauty in an effort to offset the unrealistic and unhealthy standard images associated with modeling. I was fascinated to discover that the billboard I saw was part of a series of advertisements Dove had been doing since 2004. Interestingly, one of the series asked viewers to call a toll-free number to vote whether the girls in the ad were "fab" or "fat." The results were actually posted in real time on the billboard. At one point, "fab" led the vote, with 51 percent of their viewers choosing fab over "fat." The marketing team at Dove started the Dove Self-Esteem Fund in 2006, which was established to help every girl feel positive about her looks, regardless of her size, shape, or features.

Several of the models were interviewed and asked why they had agreed to be part of such a progressive and forward-thinking campaign. Here's what some of the real, everyday fabulous women had to say:

> *I love the thought of being a part of an ad that would potentially touch many young girls to tell them that it is all right to be unique and everyone is beautiful in their own skin.*
>
> **—SHANEL LU**

" *Being a woman is beautiful. Waking up every morning and living a happy, healthy life is beautiful.* —JULIE ARKO

Young girls need to see real women like themselves in print ads or on TV.
—LINDSEY STOKES

Truth is beauty. —SIGRID SUTTER

The campaign encourages the viewer to let go of society's narrow fantastical idea of beauty and embrace beautiful reality.
—GINA CRISANTI

It's time that all women felt beautiful in their own skin. —STACI NADEAU "

I loved it! I had never seen a company take this type of risk, think outside the box, and use real women the way Dove was. I was immediately inspired to become a part of this remarkable message. When I shared my revelation with my mother, she reminded me that Dove was one of the sponsors at the upcoming annual Women's Conference she and my father host every year, which is the nation's premier forum for women.

So toward the end of my senior year I applied for an internship with Edelman Public Relations in New York, the PR firm that represented Dove, to see if I could work on the campaign and learn more about what they were doing. They normally didn't allow students who weren't already in college to intern at their firm because they usually can get college credit for their time. I wasn't starting USC until the fall, so I didn't fit the usual criteria. Even so, the agency said they'd love to have me come on board to observe and see what working in public relations was all about.

The truth is, I wasn't as interested in PR as I was in learning more about the ideas and thoughts behind this campaign. I knew this was an outstanding opportunity, so I took them up on their offer and decided to make the very most of my time in New York that summer. I did everything from running errands and packing and sending out packages to editors, to sitting in on marketing strategy meetings twice a week to observe and listen to the feedback they received on the Real Beauty campaign.

For the most part, the feedback on the campaign was positive, with women writing in thanking the company for "finally doing something like these ads." And yes, there were a few people who found the ads offensive and ugly, but those responses were mostly coming from chauvinistic men, who weren't Dove's target audience.

I believe wholeheartedly that it is so important for young girls to know their real beauty; their true beauty isn't what's on the outside but what resonates and shines from within.

I was so grateful that somebody was putting a positive twist on real beauty. The Dove ads used full-figured women, skinny girls with no curves, and average-size women to send a message to all of the girls out there who will never see images of themselves represented on the mostly Photoshopped pages of fashion magazines—images that are impossible to achieve, even if you're the model on those pages! I felt it was about time someone told women to stop striving to look like a supermodel and start embracing and rocking their own inner and outer beauty.

That summer in New York I came to realize that something else needed to be done to help spread the word and message that Dove had so brilliantly created. As a young woman, I felt I had a responsibility to do something more than just observe. I wanted to find a way to tell all of the girls and women out there who doubt themselves because they don't measure up to someone else's standard of beauty that they are *truly beautiful.* I knew there must be a way to reach girls like you and me and reassure them that they're not alone in their struggle with feeling fat, ugly, insecure, stupid, or unworthy, as I sometimes did growing up.

While it's true that other factors impact your body image and self-esteem, the majority of our cues about what we should look like come from the media. Advertising and the media feed this obsession with weight, the size of our bodies, and the constant push and reminder to be better, skinnier, prettier, perfect. There's no room for ordinary in beauty advertisements because they are selling a product that claims to be extraordinary. Still, that contributes greatly to the negative self-perception most girls have.

Because of the media, **we are under gigantic pressure to be thin and sexy,** especially when we are young, still impressionable, and susceptible to believing everything we see. The promotion of the thin, sexy ideal in our culture has created a situation where most girls and women don't like their bodies.

And who can blame them?

Body dissatisfaction can lead to all sorts of unhealthy behaviors, including eating disorders (which I will address further in chapter 4), low self-esteem, and continuous feelings of insecurity and inferiority.

It's strange and awkward to see young girls today dressed like sexy little versions of their mothers or hear them talking about what they think "sexy" is. I had different ideas of what I thought it meant to be sexy over the years, all of which were also mostly based on the images I saw in the media. None of us are immune to the power and persuasion of advertisers' messages, but in the end, sex is what sells.

I've seen so many girls change the way they dress once they develop curves in all the right places, have breasts they can show off in a low-cut top, and a booty to shake in skintight jeans. To me, that's not sexy. If you're wearing something superrevealing, there's no mystery, nothing left to the imagination. Everything is out there for the world to see. Most of the guys I talk to think girls who basically only wear clothing like their bras and underwear are classified as trashy—not sexy. There's a huge difference, girls!

I can only remember one occasion where I attempted to wear lingerie and pass it off as clothing. I put on a slip that in my mind I thought could be worn as a dress. The second I came downstairs, thinking I looked hot and ready for the night, my mother stopped me cold.

"You're not wearing that!" she said. "It's a *slip*, Katherine. It's meant to go under a dress—not be the dress." In my heart, I knew she was right, but I had seen lots of dresses that looked like slips in various magazines and on tons of girls that I knew, so I believed I could pull it off. Besides, most of the girls I was meeting that night were going to be in booty shorts and see-through tanks where you could see their bras—that's it! Comparatively speaking, I was covered up. I thought that made my outfit selection acceptable. Naturally, my mom made me change into something less revealing before I could go out for the night. At the time I hated her for making me go back upstairs and change what I thought was a great outfit, but now I thank her because all of the girls that were dressed in nearly nothing looked silly. I never made that mistake again.

I am not a big fan of the current trend in television where reality shows make girls look trashy, drunk, and slutty. Programs like *Flavor of Love, Bad Girls Club*, and even *The Bachelor* make the girls vying for the guy's attention look so desperate. Who wants to be one of twenty women trying to get the attention of one guy?

Not me!

> *On the one hand, I am quite aware that magazines and television convey an impossible standard of beauty and thinness. I realize that most women (including me) could not look like this AND hold down whatever jobs, relationships, families, etc., fill our lives. On the other hand, constantly seeing these images makes me feel subpar and that I am not good enough in the looks department.*
>
> **—KATHRYN K., CINCINNATI, OHIO**

> *Magazines project an image of an underweight model pretty much on every page emphasizing the idea that that is the norm. It makes you feel like you are abnormal or overweight if you do not look perfect.*
>
> **—CHRISTINA, WASHINGTON, D.C.**

We are bombarded by images of perfect, fat-free bodies in the pages of gossip, fashion, and teen magazines. The women on the cover of such publications represent less than .03 percent of the population! The other 99.97 percent—meaning you and me—are made to feel inferior because we don't and never will mirror that unrealistic image.

My generation was the first to grow up with twenty-four-hour access to the Internet, which meant we had non-stop contact with all sorts of information, images, and messages from the media. We spend lots of time surfing the net, checking out various Web sites, doing our own research, and developing opinions that may or may not be based on credible information. The information we see every day, whether true or not, affects us.

Girls spend hours checking out the Web, looking for photos of their favorite celebrities or the latest gossip or inspiration so they can look, dress, and be just like them. Paris Hilton, Mischa Barton, Megan Fox, and Victoria Beckham are just a few examples of celebrities who have influenced countless young girls and women who aspire to look thin. Living in a celebrity-driven culture, many of us feel as if we are on a first-name basis with people we've never met, talking about "Angelina" or "Lindsay" like they're friends of ours. The problem here is that we aren't. We see only what the media wants us to see—and often our perceptions are pretty skewed.

Let's be honest. Many of the most celebrated and recognizable women today are primarily talked about for being thin and "effortlessly beautiful." They aren't so much embraced for their *body of work* as they are for the work that goes into their bodies. The media continue to reinforce the importance of this "image" by plastering these women on the covers of most fashion magazines, not to mention every ad, billboard, and other print media we all see daily. It used to be that only models adorned the covers of fashion magazines, which made sense, because, hey, ***they're models— duh!*** They're supposed to look a certain way. But somewhere along the line, celebrities have become America's next top models, making it even harder for girls to live up to the images they are exposed to every time they open their favorite publications. The idolizing of models, actresses, and other celebrities is probably never going to go away, but we definitely have a choice in who our role models are and what it is that we admire about them.

Most girls who read fashion magazines have some idea or notion that the photos throughout the pages have been altered to some degree, but many have no idea how extensive these changes really are. For years, these "tricks" of the trade were done by using creative lighting, retouching photos, and using software that can distort the picture by making the models appear taller, thinner, more chiseled, and perfectly flawless. Computers can now basically change the way a person looks entirely. In other words, ***technology can create totally unreal humans:*** their teeth can be whitened, their hair darkened, their eyes made another color, a pimple or mole can be removed, their breasts augmented, their hips shrunken, their hair lengthened, and so on. Digital photography has made these changes even easier, although the alterations are often so apparent that they're pretty obvious. Even so, this standard creates a portrait that is not achievable by the majority of us real girls. It always makes me a little sad when I hear about someone using Photoshop on their Facebook or MySpace pages, let alone dating sites like Match.com. This practice makes it very clear that girls and women don't feel good about who they are or believe that others won't find them attractive without the same kinds of alterations to their photos that they see in magazines.

> *I think the women in magazines are gorgeous, and I always have, but now I have the sense to know they look like that because they starve themselves and because they have a team of makeup artists working on their face!*
>
> **—MOLLY, SAN FRANCISCO, CALIFORNIA**

SECRET . . . MODEL LOOK.

5 Many of the models you see in fashion magazines are between the ages of fourteen and nineteen, with the average age around sixteen. A lot of these girls haven't developed their curves yet, which is one of the reasons why they can appear so thin. Add Photoshopping into that mix and you've got a completely unattainable image.

Here's the most important thing to know when it comes to the images we see in the media—*most aren't real.* They've been altered and manipulated, which means the icon you admire doesn't even look the way she appears! The majority of these images aren't promoting self-esteem or a positive body image—they're intended to sell a product—which means they want you to feel bad about how you look by preying on your insecurities.

It is so unusual to see an unaltered photo these days that when there is one, that photo actually becomes news. I recently saw a picture of Kim Kardashian on the cover of *Life & Style* as well as eleven photos of celebrities wearing "nothing but moisturizer" featured in *People* magazine's "100 Most Beautiful" issue. I thought these images were wonderful. It made me a little sad that it is such a big deal when a celebrity decides to be seen as they really are. Maybe because I grew up in the celebrity culture I think it is normal to see celebrities when the spotlight isn't pointed directly at them. I can tell you with great certainty that most of your favorite stars are pretty ordinary when they are just living their lives. My dad is in great shape, but he isn't "pumped up" all the time. When he was acting, he prepared for a role in a film like I prepare for a presentation at school. We get ourselves ready to do the best we can and then go out there and make it happen. The celebrities you see on television and in movies are playing a role. They often train for hours a day, months in advance, to look the way they do, because it's their job. We can't all do that without seriously compromising a full and rich life. Remember, the celebrities you admire and look up to are human. They have good days and bad days, just like you and me. Don't try to live the way they do. Focus on being the best version of yourself. Go out wearing no makeup, put your hair back in a ponytail, or just wear comfy clothes. You don't have to look 100 percent all day every day. ***You can feel beautiful whenever you want.***

Plastic **Surgery**

The media does an excellent job to assure us that if we aren't happy with the way we look, "we can nip this, tuck that, suck the fat out of here, and inject it there." The message is getting through loud and clear—dangerously so.

Plastic surgery is becoming more common, and most experts believe that people, especially young girls, are starting to have plastic surgery at a younger age because of the images they see in the media.

FACT

According to the American Society for Aesthetic Plastic Surgery, the number of girls age eighteen and under who got breast implants nearly tripled from 2003 to 2004, going from 3,872 to 11,326. Most of these girls got this as their graduation present. Interesting choice of gift, girls.

Women lead the way when it comes to plastic surgery, making up 91 percent of the total procedures performed in 2008. Of those, 81,900 were cosmetic surgical procedures done on children and young adults aged thirteen to nineteen, and 271,000 were performed on young women aged twenty to twenty-nine.

The Beverly Hills Institute of Aesthetic and Reconstructive Surgery conducted a survey showing that most plastic surgery patients refer to a celebrity's feature when considering cosmetic surgery.

Most common?

- ○ Angelina Jolie lips
- ○ J. Lo's booty
- ○ Pamela Anderson's boobs

To me, altering your outer appearance isn't the answer. In fact, it's actually part of the problem. If some guy doesn't want to go out with you because you don't have big pouty fish lips, he's probably not the right guy for you anyway and is probably into you for the wrong reasons.

SECRET . . . BE NATURAL!

6 According to my guy friends, they prefer girls who don't wear a lot of makeup, who look more fresh-faced than overdone. Guys don't want a high-maintenance girl who spends hours on her hair and makeup. They want a girl they can see looking and feeling beautiful when she wakes up or just gets out of the swimming pool. Until you love yourself on the inside, you will never be happy with the image you see on the outside.

"My best friend got a nose job for her sixteenth birthday. Her nose was fine. I hate my flat chest, but I would never consider implants. I figure, there will always be someone who is prettier or thinner or smarter or has better clothes than me, but it's exhausting trying to keep up with that! I exercise because it makes me feel good about myself, and I try to eat right for my health, and I try to love the body I've been given.

—BETSY, RICHMOND, VIRGINIA

When Heidi Montag announced that by the ripe old age of twenty-three (only three years older than me!) she had undergone ten plastic surgeries, all in one day, I could hardly believe what I was hearing. I thought she looked nice the way she was before all of her procedures. I didn't understand the extreme makeover she felt she needed. Interestingly, when she went public with her admission, most of the reports failed to mention that just two years earlier, she had already had a nose job, got collagen injections in her lips, and had a breast augmentation.

Thirteen surgeries in two years?

Is it me, or does that seem a little over the top?

There is something fundamentally wrong when a beautiful twenty-three-year-old girl goes to such an extreme to change herself to look like someone else.

Was the media pressure too much for her?

Did her husband somehow coerce her into it?

I have a lot more questions than answers on this one.

Out of curiosity, I looked up what exactly she had done.

Here's the list: a mini brow lift, nose job, her ears pinned back, fat injections in her cheeks and lips, a buttocks augmentation, liposuction to her waist and thighs, a revision to her previous breast augmentation, a chin reduction, liposuction to her neck, and Botox.

This got me wondering.

Is Heidi unique or is having cosmetic plastic surgery a growing trend for girls?

Perhaps we only know about hers because she is a public figure, while thousands of young girls are undergoing similar procedures every day?

Heidi is unique in one way. She can afford to have that many surgeries, but she is hardly alone in her obsession to look perfect, even if it means enduring multiple and painful cosmetic procedures. The media play one of the biggest roles in pushing girls like Heidi with images of unattainable perfection. When she was interviewed about her decision to have the surgeries, Heidi said she never got over being teased about her looks when she was younger. She said she hated seeing herself on TV with two flaps sticking out of the sides of her head, which made her feel that she looked like "Dumbo." She now describes her former flaps as "sexy ears," which she is proud of now, so she "can wear her hair in an up-do instead of hiding her ears behind her hair."

Sexy . . . *ears?*

What does that even mean? *I was unaware ears could be sexy!*

So here's the deal. While Heidi may have gone to an extreme, sadly she represents a large population of girls who are willing to do anything to be seen as pretty. Beautiful girls have self-esteem issues too! Confidence has a whole lot more to do with attitude than with looks. I think some of the most gorgeous women, including Sarah Jessica Parker and Julia Roberts, are not always considered to be classically pretty, but they are nevertheless beautiful because they are attractive, smart, and interesting too!

To be totally fair, I do think there are times when plastic surgery may be a smart alternative for some girls. There are some procedures that are done for more than purely cosmetic reasons. For some girls, a minor procedure that helps them feel better about their appearance, such as having their ears pinned, a nose job, or a cleft lip repaired are understandable. I am not against plastic surgery, especially when it is a life-threatening issue, but I do feel it has gone to an extreme with girls having multiple elective and mostly unnecessary surgeries.

CRAZY COSMETIC
trend!

Umbilicoplasty: the reconstruction and reshaping of one's belly button to look more attractive. Let's make a note: all belly buttons are weird! They are not meant to be an attractive feature one must show to people every day. It'd be one thing if your belly button was on your face, but it's under your shirt most of the time. So calm down, girls!

While research has shown that people who have plastic surgery are happier after their procedures, most don't actually feel better about themselves down the road. For the most part, people who have plastic surgery to augment their looks don't see drastic changes in their overall beauty. I believe that in the end, even if you improve your outer beauty, without inner beauty, you will never really be happy and secure with who you are.

And there is a downside to having any type of surgery, especially elective surgery. Complications can include:

✔ infections
✔ a botched outcome
✔ and in some cases, even death during or afterward

Usher's ex-wife went into a coma after hours of cosmetic surgery, and Heidi Montag has even admitted to difficulties waking up. She was put on oxygen to help regulate her breathing until she was fully recovered. Former Miss Argentina Solange Magnano suffered a pulmonary embolism and died after going under the knife. These are just a few examples of the unexpected dangers you can face during or after plastic surgery.

After my appendix burst during my first year of college, I can tell you one thing—I will never in my life voluntarily have surgery! I was in so much pain and agony after having my appendix removed, I can't even imagine how crazy it would be to have something bigger done voluntarily to your body.

"Removing thin women from television/ magazines and putting 'normal' women in their place would certainly help, but changing parents' and young girls' attitudes toward achievement may be more effective. What I mean is, mothers could point out smart, career-driven, or otherwise accomplished women and say, 'Now isn't she cool? I think so! I would love to be like her,' to teach their daughters to recognize and respect other forms of achievement outside of beauty. Girls who feel accomplished in other ways probably won't feel the pressure to be beautiful that most women do.

—MOLLY, SAN FRANCISCO, CALIFORNIA

Rock What You've Got Women

Role models are people you respect, admire, and look up to. They set a good example by choosing to live their lives in a way that not only inspires but also empowers others. There's a great need for more positive role models these days. Today's young women need more role models who are smart, confident, sophisticated, and realistically beautiful. There are far too many images in the media of role models who take zero responsibility for their actions and don't end up paying the price for their decisions. The media sends the wrong message when they cover these girls who don't take responsibility for their lives and live without either good values or moral judgments. If the media would abstain from promoting these images of women who are gaining fame for sex tapes and over-the-top behavior and instead focus on women who are doing things in the world that make a difference in the lives of others, then that would inspire the rest of us. We would no longer have to hold ourselves accountable for how we look but could then start to appreciate what we bring to the table, and how we could bring change to our communities and even the world.

Women including first lady Michelle Obama, Oprah, Cindy Crawford, Beyoncé, Kelly Clarkson, Alicia Keys, Eva Longoria, Jessica Simpson, Danica Patrick, Taylor Swift, and most special to me, my mother, Maria Shriver, are all good examples of women who embrace their real inner and outer beauty. They're all authentic, smart, beautiful, and successful women who promote the advancement of young girls to believe they can do and be anything they dream. These women are all **Rock What You've Got women.**

Who are some of your role models?

Take a second to ask yourself who, in your life, inspires you?

Who empowers you?

Who do you look up to?

For most of us, the most important role models in our lives are our parents. We will always look up to them to teach, protect, advise, and guide us throughout our lives. I am one of the lucky girls in this world who grew up in a home with parents who love me, care about me, and only want the best for all of their children. I have two working parents who somehow seemed to juggle it all—making it look downright easy most of the time while I struggled simply to keep up with my schoolwork, get in a workout between classes, eat, sleep, and most important, *have fun!*

Regardless of their schedules, my parents always made time to be present in my life—this is especially true for my mother, who did a remarkable job finessing the various hats she wore throughout the years. Her number one role in life, however, was and still is seeing to the well-being of her children.

Let me be totally honest. My mom wasn't one of the "cool" moms. Though she always made it easy for me to talk to her about anything by welcoming me with open arms and being nonjudgmental, she was by no means a pushover. She made sure to play the role of my mom, not my girlfriend. And as a result of her sometimes tough and unconditional love, she has become my very best friend in life.

My mother was very firm with me growing up. In fact, she was the strictest mom among my group of friends. She made it very clear what was acceptable and unacceptable behavior, and I was expected to adhere to her rules. There was no debating, no negotiating. It was her way or the highway, and I mean that in the best way possible. There were plenty of times over the years I thought I hated my mom's stupid rules. We would get into fights about them and I would always wind up not understanding why she was making my life what I considered to be a living hell. I thought she was mean and coldhearted for giving me a curfew to be home by midnight. While other friends were allowed to have coed sleepovers, my parents would just laugh if I tried to bring up the subject. "It will never happen," they said. As for school, my parents didn't care about coming home with straight As or Bs, but there was no leniency for laziness. As long as I was trying my hardest, they were satisfied. Still, there were plenty of times I studied hard and didn't make the grade.

To make things even more challenging, once my dad was elected governor of California, I was constantly followed by a local police officer, which made it impossible to get away with anything anyway.

Try outrunning a police officer who is constantly on your tail!

It's not easy, but . . . it can be done . . . sometimes!

(I would tell you how I did it, but I don't want to give away my methods just yet, as I have two younger brothers who still have to figure these things out for themselves!)

Choosing not to disappoint my parents inevitably meant I was letting down my friends. I knew my parents didn't want me drinking alcohol or doing drugs. And yet so many of my friends were trying to get me to go there.

I think one of the reasons I was able to get through my high school years and come out the other side a relatively sane person was because of the strong relationship I have with my parents and siblings. I may not have known it at the time, but the best thing I had in high school was my relationship with my parents, and especially with my mom. If you can't at the very least share your thoughts with your mom, and ask her questions about becoming a woman, you won't be able to learn from her experiences about what you will be going through. *Figuring it out on your own can be very lonely.*

Bottom line, you and your mom are both women. You will go through the same changes she did. Why not use this time in your life to develop a stronger relationship with your mom? If you're planning on going off to college or striking out on your own, this is the only time you'll have when you'll be at home and can bond with her. In a couple of years (or even now, for some of you) you'll be out there creating your own life. You won't need to speak to your parents every single day, but it will be great to know you have their unconditional love and support and the freedom to call them up and ask them questions.

I understand that may be a challenge for those of you who may have moms who aren't present, interested, or are a little off the deep end. And that's okay. If you find you can't or don't want to talk to your mom, find someone who you respect and admire and talk to her. Try to talk to an older sister, an aunt, a cousin, or a close family friend who you trust. You want to pick a responsible adult who has it going on, someone who can be a good role model and will share her experiences with you. Find someone who you can relate to and feel you can tell anything to.

I had lots of friends who couldn't talk with their moms like I do with mine. So my mom became the "go to" mom for those girls. They would ask her questions about boyfriend troubles, about their parents not understanding them, and about any other topic that young girls deal with while growing up. It made me a little sad to know my friends didn't share their true feelings with their own moms, but I was happy they could vent and get it all out with someone like my mom, because she genuinely cared about them as if they were her kids too. She taught them that *it is okay to be honest with your feelings* because we all do have feelings and sometimes we just want someone to listen to them. If you keep them bottled up, one day there will be a giant volcanic eruption of emotions. We can't ignore our feelings or they will develop into something much bigger than annoying little boyfriend issues or hating the size of your thighs. (See chapter 4, which discusses eating disorders.)

> *My father could not care less and thinks I'm beautiful inside and out. But my mother could lay off the criticism a bit! At the same time, she also berates me for not having enough self-confidence, which is ironic.*
>
> **—RACHEL, NEW YORK, NEW YORK**

> *I think in fifth or sixth grade I noticed my dad giving me looks and I knew how he was obsessed with appearances. So, I got the idea that whatever he was looking at wasn't pretty. I think they just want me to be happy, but as I have grown older, I feel as if when they look at me they are either embarrassed by my appearance or think I am fat.*
>
> **—CHRISTINA, WASHINGTON, D.C.**

FOR MOMS ONLY

According to Renee Hobbs, EdD, associate professor of communications at Temple University, "The average teen girl gets about 180 minutes of media exposure a day and, on average, about ten minutes of parental interaction." Now that you have read that, try to make it home for a family dinner or a check-in chat with your daughter. It's important!

Parents have to take the time to be with their children, to participate in their lives and encourage their kids. Parents are their children's most important role models. If they aren't around to set a good example for their kids, the likelihood is they'll search elsewhere and end up making the wrong choices and decisions they'll regret.

In my family, we had no choice about whether or not we would attend family dinners. Every night at 7:00 sharp, we were all expected to be sitting at the dinner table together so we could enjoy a family meal. We spent the entire time going around the table check-ing in with one another, one by one, talking about what we did that day or any dilemma or drama we were dealing with at the moment. Back then, I thought it was annoying to have to wait for all of us to congregate together before we could eat dinner. To this day, my brother moans and groans about how long dinner takes. I later realized the importance of having a distinct time to catch up and bond as a family. It is really important to share this type of intimacy with your family to keep your relationships strong.

It's imperative that parents don't give mixed messages to their kids, especially if they are battling their own self-esteem and body image issues. Mothers are especially susceptible to inadvertently passing along their hang-ups about their bodies to their daughters. Girls are heavily influenced by the behavior their mothers demonstrate, so they notice if their mom is always on a diet, exercises obsessively, and makes negative statements about her appearance. If you have a tendency to rely on cosmetic procedures to keep a youthful appearance, chances are your daughter will grow up believing that this is what she should do too. A mother is her daughter's first and most influential role model.

A father should also watch what he says to his daughter, because the way she relates to other men often mirrors her relationship with her dad. A father should avoid talking about his daughter's physical appearance in a negative way. In fact, he really needs to be aware of how he responds to women in general, because that influences his daughter's perception of how men see women. As obvious as it may seem, it is not in your daughter's best interest to hear her father talk about how sexy, hot, pretty, thin, or desirable his favorite celebrity is. These comments only reinforce your daughter's idea that you will love her, think she's pretty or as good as those women only if she looks like them too. Listen up, dads, because your daughters are listening to you!

SECRET ... DADS CAN BE CLUELESS.

7 Girls talk about their dads and their relationship with their dads. Fathers should watch how they treat their wives and other women. If you don't find yourself spending time with your dad, ask for it. Because in reality, most of them are clueless.

Compliments are one of the

best ways parents can help build their daughter's self-image
and self-esteem. If you tell her she looks pretty or that she's
doing so well in school, it will surely put a smile on her face.
Show your daughters images of girls who have healthy body
images rather than tell them. Give them examples of positive
role models they can aspire to be like. *Healthy* doesn't
always translate into words, especially if your daughter
thinks the superthin waiflike next top model is "healthy."

If you teach your daughters to surround themselves
with people who make them feel good instead of those who
reinforce their insecurities, they will quickly discover that
the support of these friends is the absolute best method for
fighting against self-doubt. Offer compliments as often as
you can. Giving them feels as good as getting them. Not
only will you help your daughter feel better about herself,
but you will also be teaching her the value of giving compliments to others too.

Make an effort to watch television together with your
kids so you can discuss the images they are being exposed
to. Becoming a witness to these messages will help you
better understand the pressures young girls face about their
body image in today's media-driven world. This exercise
will help parents explain how unrealistic these images are
and the importance of loving their inner and outer beauty.

CHAPTER 4

Extreme Measures

what you need to *know* about eating *disorders*

> **FACT**
>
> Five to ten million girls in the United States have an eating disorder. One out of four college-aged women have an eating disorder.

When I was in seventh

grade, someone telling me "You're so skinny" felt a little awkward. I always said "Thanks?" with a question mark at the end because I was never sure if they were being kind or critical. I wasn't looking for people to think I was thin—at least not in seventh grade!

One of my best friends at the time was the super skinniest girl I knew. Her body was completely different from mine. ***I was naturally curvy;*** she was naturally thin. She could eat whatever she wanted, even a Snickers bar and midnight snacks, and never ever gain a pound. She was so slim that her hip bones actually popped out of the top of her low-rider jeans. She once told me that guys love when they can see girls' hip bones—that it was sexy to be *that* skinny. Naturally I believed her and thought what she was saying had to be true, so I did everything I could to get my hip bones to poke out too.

She and I had an ongoing competition all through seventh and partially into eighth grade, where we challenged each other to keep our weight below ninety-six pounds. I was five feet eight inches at the time, tall for a girl my age. I've always been naturally competitive, so when my friend challenged me to keep my weight under ninety-six pounds, I took it very seriously. If I am challenged to do something, I'm in it—to win it. End of story. I had to work extra hard to keep my weight at or below hers, but I did it. Her obsession became my obsession.

> *Over the summers, kids used to look at me and call me a 'whale' when I was in a bathing suit. Others, including my parents, used to tell me to stop eating when I wasn't finished with a meal. I was also called 'fat' multiple times. I will never forget these comments for as long as I live.*
>
> **—CHRISTINA, WASHINGTON, D.C.**

Without realizing the risk to my health or having any clue about what I was doing to my body, I literally starved myself, eating only when absolutely necessary and ignoring everyone's comments that I looked pale, thin, and unwell. I look back at photos of me from those years and can now see I was too skinny. But at the time, I thought I looked beautiful.

When I went to the doctor for my annual checkup that year, he told me I needed to eat more—that I was too thin for my build. He tried to be sly by asking me if eating made me feel bad or guilty, clearly trying to discern if I had an eating disorder or some type of body dysmorphia. I emphatically assured him that *eating* did not make me feel bad. And though I didn't share with the doctor the real reason why I wasn't eating, it was pretty simple; for me, it was nothing more than a friendly competition with my best friend to be skinnier than she was. I saw a lot of girls my age doing things like this, so I didn't realize there was anything wrong with our seemingly innocent pact.

Was it wise?

No!

Is it real?

Does it happen?

All the time.

I don't think I would have been as obsessed with my body if not for my friend. ***Peer pressure is very powerful and easy to give in to.*** The first time I realized I had protruding hip bones, I finally felt like I fit in because I was just like my friend. Of course, our bodies were completely different. She had one of those insane bodies where she could eat anything and never gain an ounce, the kind of body and metabolism that everyone envies. But I had to give up so much to look like she did. It wasn't until my friend was abruptly taken out of school to go "away" that I realized she had a real problem and that what we were doing to our bodies was unhealthy. Her reason for disappearing was confusing to me because we never spoke after she left. I had heard through the grapevine that she was being sent away for treatment, even though her parents insisted on telling everyone they were simply moving.

It never dawned on me that what we were doing was a bad thing. I now recognize how serious the situation was and how much worse it could have become.

I didn't think much about anyone's body until I began paying attention to my own. But by the time I reached my senior year of high school, I began to notice that the majority of girls in the middle school were all super skinny. They all wore straight-legged jeans and tiny, midriff baring tight tops, which made them look like a bundle of toothpicks standing together in the hallways. They were all so tiny, for the most part flat chested, wore quite a bit of makeup, and had long, straightened hair. Even the girls with naturally wavy or curly hair wore theirs straight. I'm not sure when those girls got up in the morning to blow out their hair so they could make it to school on time, but it must have taken them hours to get ready. Looking at those girls made me sad. I couldn't help but feel a little sorry that they were so caught up in their bodies and looks. I wanted to take them all aside and let them know that it doesn't matter what you look like in seventh grade! No one cares! I look back on my seventh grade pictures and laugh at the outfits I wore and how I chose to do my hair. **We're all awkward at thirteen!** I wanted to tell them that they will have years to worry about clothes and makeup. Enjoy this carefree time in your life.

Dissatisfaction with your body can start at a very young

age and, if not handled properly, can and often does lead to eating disorders. According to research in "Causes of Eating Disorders" in the *Annual Review of Psychology,* as many as ***"ten million females (and one million males)*** are fighting a life and death battle with an eating disorder such as anorexia or bulimia in the United States. Millions more are struggling with binge eating disorder."

Girls and women between the ages of fifteen and twenty-nine are most at risk, with bulimia patients outnumbering anorexia patients by at least two to one.

I asked Susan Walker, of the Walker Wellness Clinic in Dallas, Texas, a leading treatment center for anyone suffering from a diagnosed eating disorder, to share her latest information on the subject. She is on the front lines, and I wondered if she thought things were getting better or worse.

"We have noticed a more recent trend in terms of admission for outpatient treatment to have increased among young female adults with anorexia nervosa and bulimia nervosa between the ages of eighteen to thirty and particularly college-aged students. We have also seen the prevalence of partial eating disorders, meaning they fulfill some but not all of the criteria for the disorder, at least twice that of full-symptom eating disorders," Susan observed.

The numbers appear to be growing, which makes it so important for you to get all the facts before you fall into this type of behavior.

Anorexia, Bulimia, and Binge Eating

By the time I reached ninth grade, my awareness of eating disorders had been heightened thanks to my friend who had been sent away. My school showed all ninth graders a film that focused on the topic in our sex ed class. After we watched that movie, an older girl who was a senior at our school came to talk to my class about her eating disorder. She discussed her anorexia and bulimia as well as her longtime troubles battling depression and thoughts of suicide. She even showed us her cut marks on her wrists, something I've never forgotten. She talked about how she used to feel like she was in a really dark place and totally out of control. At one time, she really hated her life.

She shared a lot of intimate secrets with us from her past, saying in order to feel something, anything, she used to make herself throw up or cut herself. She talked about how she felt numb to pain and to the world.

After getting help, she now understood that you can have a good body without having these eating disorders that she struggled with. At the end of her presentation, she told the class that if we ever felt like we needed someone to talk to or if we felt like we were battling these feelings ourselves that she would be there to listen and give us advice.

It was an effective approach to teach us about the dangers of anorexia and bulimia, although whenever I saw the older girl around school, I never thought of her as anything other than "the one with the eating disorder." Probably not the tag she was looking for, I am sure. But she made me think long and hard when any thoughts of bingeing or purging ever crossed my mind.

Although an eating disorder may start off being about weight and food, it's usually about much deeper and more emotional issues. An eating disorder can start with a crash diet and quickly turn into bingeing, purging, and starving as a way to cope with your feelings or feel some sense of control over your life.

The American Psychiatric Association defines *anorexia nervosa* as "a disturbance in the way in which one's body weight or shape is experienced; undue influence of body weight or shape on self-evaluation, or denial of the seriousness of current low body weight." You can tell if someone is suffering from anorexia if she has a sudden and drastic drop in weight, maintains her weight at an unhealthy level below her normal weight, eats very little or skips meals altogether, won't eat in front of others, wears loose-fitting clothes to hide her skeletal body, exercises frequently, may have stopped getting her period, thinks and says she is too fat when she is obviously not, and makes excuses to avoid eating.

When I went to Costa Rica in the ninth grade, one of the girls traveling with our group was bulimic. One night after a bunch of girls had had a huge dinner and felt as if our food was stuffed up to our throats, this girl took us to the bathroom and tried to teach five of us how to stick our fingers down our throats and make ourselves throw up. We were all gaining weight from eating our steady diet of freshly baked bread and tortillas. It seemed like an easy solution. Despite her best efforts, one of my friends and I couldn't seem to go through with it.

At some point in life, I think most girls contemplate making themselves throw up after a big meal. Even if you're not serious about it, you've probably thought about doing it. I know I have, but I never went through with it because I can't stand the idea of throwing up. I never understood why anyone would puke on purpose. I've had food poisoning a couple of times in my life. I thought that was the absolute worst feeling in the world. I could never intentionally make myself feel that way. Sadly, there are those girls out there who not only go through with the deed but also become addicted to it.

Throwing up is not a solution to overeating, losing weight, or controlling your body issues. It is a very serious symptom that something much bigger is going on—bulimia nervosa. This disorder is when someone overeats and then purges their food by vomiting. According to the American Psychiatric Association, the diagnostic criteria for bulimia nervosa include self-evaluation that is "unduly influenced by body shape and weight. Someone who suffers from bulimia has frequent weight fluctuations, spends a lot of time in the bathroom, especially after meals, eats a significant amount of food and never seems to gain weight, exercises all the time as a way to compensate for overeating, has irregular periods or misses getting her period, and possibly uses laxatives on a regular basis."

Binge eating is defined as compulsive eating without vomiting. Someone who suffers from this feels out of control around and about food. She cannot help herself when it comes to eating. She plans her life around eating and food. She will often eat in private, sneaking snacks that are loaded with calories and fat. A binge eater consumes a vast quantity of food quickly. She will eat in excess of 2,500 calories or more in one sitting at least two times a week.

How Do *Eating Disorders* Start?

FACT

Anorexia and bulimia appear to be more prevalent in industrialized countries. These disorders are most common in the United States, Canada, Europe, Australia, Japan, New Zealand, and South Africa, but little systematic work has examined prevalence in other cultures.

There is no "one thing" that triggers the onset of an eating disorder. It is usually a combination of factors. According to Susan Walker, "genetics (perfectionism/OCD traits/anxiety), pressures for thinness, and gender (female) all contribute. Outside factors include: puberty, life stressors, peer pressure, and media messages."

Most experts agree that the earlier the intervention for treating eating disorders occurs, the better chance for recovery. Early diagnosis and treatment can minimize body image distortions so the patient can return to seeing herself as "normal."

Craig Johnson, PhD, a prominent eating disorders expert at Laureate Hospital, says that "genetic predispositions load the gun and what actually pulls the trigger to start the onset of the eating disorder is stress or situations such as trauma, for example the loss of a loved one, divorce, or even date rape."

Susan Walker has observed this at her wellness center over the past twenty-eight years. Chronic stress, a significant or profound loss such as the breakup of a relationship, divorce in the family, loss of a loved one or animal, feelings of powerlessness and losing control over situations, trauma such as date rape, rape, molestation, or any type of sexual abuse, depression, anxiety that may lead to panic attacks, chronic worrying, and obsessive-compulsive tendencies are all potential triggers.

There is so much social pressure put on girls to look a certain way and have a perfect body. What this boils down to, girls, is that an eating disorder can develop as a result of being unhappy with how you think your body appears and from having low self-esteem, depression, anxiety, anger, loneliness, or just the desire and need to fit in. They can start if there's trouble at home or school, a history of being teased about your weight or size, and even from sexual abuse. Dissatisfaction with body size or shape appears to be one of the best predictors of behavior that can ultimately lead to an eating disorder.

Our emotions drive each of us and directly affect how we approach food and eating. Home life is a big piece when it comes to why girls turn to bingeing, purging, and closet eating. My relationship to food was impacted by my home environment—especially as I transformed from a little girl to a teenager.

Growing up the daughter of Arnold Schwarzenegger made me more aware of my body. There are pictures of my dad in his prime as a bodybuilder all over the gym in our house. I have even seen posters of him posing in various other places outside the walls of our home, so there's never really been any escaping the idea of his perfect physique.

Whenever I worked out with Dad growing up, he was very focused on teaching me the *right* way to do various exercises. At the time it felt like he was being hypercritical of me, but looking back now, I understand he was just trying to help me so I would know how to correctly do things, such as lifting weights, so I wouldn't get hurt.

My dad was very extreme in his eating habits, something that stemmed from his early days as a bodybuilder. When he was training for a movie, he was extremely disciplined about food. If he was fasting or eating a high-protein diet, he watched all of us like a hawk, virtually policing every bite of food we ate. Of course, we were just kids, so our eating habits weren't as strict as his, but he always expected us to make healthy choices.

My mom grew up in a house where her mother was very weight conscious. My grandma was five feet nine inches tall and weighed less than one hundred pounds for most of her adult life. When we'd go to lunch or dinner with her, she would usually order something like toast and honey.

She was very skinny and quite strict about food when my mother was growing up, which made my mom very aware of her own relationship with food when it came to us kids. Mom never forced us to eat or to stop eating. She had gone through her own phases of fluctuations in her weight as a teen and into her twenties and didn't want to influence any of her kids when it came to food and dieting. When she went to college, she gained weight like most of us do. She didn't lose her extra weight until she was hired to be on television. A producer told her she needed to lose *twenty pounds* before he'd let her appear on the air, and she did it and did it fast! I'm sure you've heard the saying that "the camera adds ten pounds." I can't imagine dropping twenty pounds, but she did it. She kept up healthy eating habits after that and changed her lifestyle. All she wanted for her kids was for us to be healthy.

I think my mom empathized with me when I was struggling with my weight. She had experienced her own mother passing along her unhealthy relationship with food, and my mom wanted to break that cycle with me and my sister, so she never policed us. My dad was more the one in our house monitoring everything we ate, asking, **"Do you really want to eat that?"** and "Are you sure you need that second helping?" I know my dad didn't ask us these annoying questions to be mean, he was just trying to watch out for us.

Questions like this created an intense feeling of anger in me, which ultimately formulated how I began to feel about food. Some people eat when they're bored, depressed, anxious, or angry, while others reject food altogether.

A healthy relationship with food and eating is characterized by the ability to recognize and respond to hunger and stopping when you are full. It is also the absence of fear, and acceptance that all foods are allowed in moderation.

Despite the awareness my friends and I had of the dangers, I knew lots of girls growing up who battled anorexia and bulimia or both. For some it was a dangerous passing phase. For a few unfortunate girls, it was something far more. I witnessed these girls firsthand as they ruined their bodies and will likely suffer lifelong negative effects from their behavior. Some girls corroded all of their teeth from throwing up, while another I knew wrecked her metabolism with her dangerous eating habits. To be certain, when taken to extremes, the effects of an eating disorder are not a pretty picture. You might think you look good in that moment, but you won't be looking so hot when you seem to be aging at a much faster rate than your friends as well as experiencing some serious health issues such as

FACT

According to Dr. Linn Goldberg, MD, head of health promotion and sports medicine with the Oregon Health and Science University in Portland, Oregon, in 2004, nearly one-third of all teen girls were taking "body shaping" diet pills to get thin.

✔ hair loss,
✔ brittle bones,
✔ rotting teeth,
✔ poor metabolism, and
✔ respiratory problems,
    just to name a few!

CALLING THE
food police

It seems as though everyone always has an opinion about what food we should or should not eat. We hear these messages in the media, read them in magazines, and watch them on television. The one place that should be safe from these messages is inside your home. Many parents take on the role of telling their child what they can or cannot eat. Although their motive is to be helpful and to try to guide their child to eat healthier and make better choices, the action of "food policing" is a lose-lose situation for everyone, especially for your child, so just don't do it.

Food policing is the action of commenting on everything your child eats. Believe me, if your daughter is eating a doughnut, she's probably aware that it isn't the best choice she could be making—especially if she is battling her weight. When parents continually comment on their child's eating habits, it inevitably leads to the child developing a complex about food. This is not in anyone's best interest.

Food policing can take place among friends too. When your best friend tells you to back away from the cookies or bag of chips or brings up what you ate the day before, she's monitoring your food consumption. Some friends will tell you for your own good, while other girls may say something bitchy to make you feel bad or guilty. In my high school, most of the girls never ate in front of the boys. We'd drink Diet Coke and pretend we weren't hungry, when in fact, most of us were **very** hungry. We were too afraid that boys would watch us eat, wonder why we were eating that, and then think we definitely didn't need to be eating.

My friends were pretty good about not being overly obvious with the food policing, but there were a few times when certain friends would indulge in a cookie or some other treat when we got back late from a party. My super-body-conscious friends would glare at them with a stare like: "How could you!?"

I had one friend in particular who was really thin and always gave people a hard time for eating sweets because she totally believed it would go right to our thighs and she wanted to "help us." For her, it was the opposite, or so she claimed. She always bragged about how she could eat whatever she wanted and not gain a single pound! (Rub it in our face, why don't you!)

One day it occurred to me that she was lying because she never let herself have a treat or indulge in anything. She would just watch us eat a cookie and give us a judgmental glare. I didn't care because I knew we were all having more fun with our lives than she was.

I think part of your week should include a little treat. You can't always follow the rules with everything, especially eating. So once a week, give yourself a "cheat day" or a reward with an "I was really good this week" day. We are only human, and if you eat a cookie tonight, I assure you, it won't kill you. You can go to the gym tomorrow and work it off. So relax and enjoy life a little!

As for those glaring eyes from your friends?

Glare right back with an "I'll bet you're jealous you're not eating this delicious, yummy, gooey cookie" stare.

The *Danger* of Diet Pills and Laxatives

One trend that has sadly caught on is the use of laxatives and diet pills as a method of losing or controling weight. The use of diet pills has been pushed to the mainstream by people like the late Anna Nicole Smith, who is among a long list of celebrities who have endorsed diet pills that are "guaranteed" to get results. Ironically, most advertisements for these products are followed by a disclaimer that states "results not typical." They also don't disclose the dangers, especially to young girls whose bodies are not mature enough to endure the duress and stress these seemingly harmless helpers place on our systems. Our younger years are critical, especially to us girls, because that's when our bones are being built. Diet pills can affect the development of our bones, which can have a long-term impact, especially as we age.

Who wants to have brittle bones?

Not me!

And trust me, neither do you!

In 2007, the U.S. Food and Drug Administration discovered sixty-nine different over-the-counter weight-loss supplements, including those marked as natural and herbal, that contained potent pharmaceutical ingredients that can cause serious health complications, including seizures and strokes. Hidden ingredients are just one of the problems when assessing the dangers of taking diet pills. The reason the manufacturer can get away with hiding these ingredients is because over-the-counter diet pills are not regulated by the government, which means there's no one validating or verifying the safety of the content of the pills or the consequences of taking them.

Metabolism-boosting pills will suppress your appetite, but they will also increase your blood pressure and heart rate to very dangerous levels. If you have a history of heart palpitations, a weakened heart, or other cardiovascular concerns, diet pills can be deadly. Dr. Laurie Mitan, MD, an associate professor at Cincinnati Children's Hospital Medical Center in Ohio, warns, "We've had teens hospitalized in our ICU with cardiac ischemia after using diet pills just one time!" So hear this: just like you *can* get pregnant the first time you have unprotected sex, you *can* also suffer severe if not lethal consequences from taking a single diet pill. My advice is to leave them alone. **Walk away** from the temptation to take the easy "fix" when it comes to your weight. It'll be temporary, and if you're not careful it could cost you.

I wasn't the girl in school who never gave in to peer pressure. My parents gave me a strong foundation to say no whenever I found myself in a situation where I didn't feel comfortable. But that doesn't mean I didn't experiment with things.

For me, peer pressure was ever present in high school. Now that I am in college, I don't really feel it as much. I was always pretty good at standing my ground, but when I was out at a party with friends, especially the first few times I was allowed to go, and everyone around me was telling me to have a sip of a drink, I couldn't help but give in to it.

There were several occasions where people were

telling me to try this drink or drug where I was able to say no. But people started making fun of me, calling me "innocent" and "little miss perfect," so I felt pressured to do something about it. I have to admit that being called those names made me make some decisions I am not proud of. There were some things I was way too scared to mess around with, and I struggled to follow my values and fit in at the same time. I was very blessed to have an older girlfriend to talk to who had been there and back herself. She would tell me to trust her, that it just was not worth it. Believe it or not, I found myself watching kids I knew taking things too far and ending up in rehab.

It didn't take me long to realize that drinking was not for me. I am one of those people who can have fun without getting drunk. I usually wound up being the designated driver for my friends in high school. At the time, I was actually kind of upset about being tagged as the official DD, but it was better than getting into a car with someone who had been drinking.

Let's face it. ***Peer pressure is tough and real,*** and sometimes you just can't help but give in. We are all only human, and it is a natural process to go through, especially in high school and college. Peer pressure is a really hard thing to avoid and an even harder thing to be around. Listen to your gut feelings in those situations. You may feel like a loser for not trying something in the moment, but think about the aftermath of the situation and the potential negative consequences. Take one moment before you take a drink or hit of something and really consider the possibilities if you get caught, or worse, hurt someone else or yourself. In the end, you will be in a much better place for choosing not to participate. And remember, above all, *if you are with friends who didn't say no, don't get into the car with them.* Call your parents or catch a ride with someone else.

Though drugs and alcohol were never a real issue for me, my biggest pressure in high school was managing my weight. There were lots of kids in my school who were obsessed with staying thin. The easiest and most prevalent method other kids were using to lose weight was a drug called Adderall.

Girls are experimenting with this drug and seeing quick and significant changes in their weight by taking it. Adderall is a commonly abused prescription medication that is particularly popular with high school and college students. This prescription drug is very easy to get, and those who are aware of its weight-loss benefits can access it simply by going to their physician and telling him or her they are having a hard time focusing, concentrating in class, and retaining information. The doctor runs a couple of tests, diagnoses the patient with ADHD, and writes the prescription. It's really that simple. I find this trend frightening because so many of my peers have turned to Adderall as a simple alternative to dieting and exercise. But using it is very dangerous. Some people even snort it to stay awake when they're studying for an exam or out late partying. If you aren't supposed to be taking this drug for ADHD, you risk the possibility of stroke, heart attack, high blood pressure, and other cardiovascular problems.

Another popular diet method is to use laxatives, which can be easily purchased over the counter. Laxative abuse occurs when a person attempts to get rid of unwanted calories, lose weight, or feel thin or empty through the repeated use of laxatives. This practice is often used in conjunction with eating binges as a way to try to move the food through the digestive system before it can be absorbed. Unfortunately, this doesn't really work. The "empty" or skinny feeling is actually the loss of water weight, which returns as soon as you drink any fluids. Long-term use of laxatives can cause a dependency, which means your colon may stop reacting to the dose you're taking and will require a larger dose to produce a bowel movement. If that happens, you could suffer from internal organ damage, including a lazy colon, colon infection, irritable bowel syndrome, and even colon cancer. Misusing laxatives, even herbal ones like senna, is a potentially dangerous and unhealthy weight-loss method.

Diet pills don't affect the unhealthy choices you make when it comes to eating. It's a temporary weight-loss fix that won't last the second after you stop taking them. The only way to achieve a healthy weight is to make changes to your entire lifestyle, including the foods you eat, and increasing the amount of exercise you do daily. **There's no magic pill** that will give you lasting, healthy results. If you exercise and eat healthful foods, you will be fine. Like all goals in life, you get the most success when you challenge yourself to reach it responsibly.

" *I remember a time having a sense of helplessness over a friend's weight. In high school, I found out she had become anorexic, and after speaking to a trusted teacher about what I should do, confronted her about it. Fortunately, the situation was eventually resolved.*

—AUDREY, ZANESVILLE, OHIO "

Susan Walker offered some

advice on what you should do if you suspect you or someone you know may be suffering from an eating disorder. She explained that sometimes parents may be the last to know that an eating disorder has set in, because girls camouflage their bodies by wearing oversize clothes and parents aren't always cognizant of the bingeing-purge cycles, food restricting, excessive exercise, fasting, diuretics, or laxative abuse.

Due to the shame and embarrassment, someone who

is battling an eating disorder often avoids seeking treatment. But if both parents and patient know what to look for, they may be able to prevent the onset of an eating disorder.

One way to help your child eat well and help you worry less is

to know what your job is and what your child's job is when it comes to eating. Some food experts call this the division of responsibility. If your child only wants to eat one type of food, he or she is doing the parent's job of deciding what food choices are. In the division of responsibility, it is the parent's job to decide what foods are offered.

The division of responsibility is outlined below:

- ➡ Your job is to offer nutritious food choices at meals and snack times. You decide the what, where, and when of eating.
- ➡ Your child's job is to choose how much he or she will eat of the foods you serve, NOT YOU. Your child decides how much or even whether to eat.

If this idea is new to you, it may take a little time for both you and your child to adjust. In time, your child will learn that he or she will be allowed to eat as little or as much as he or she wants at each meal and snack. This will encourage your child to continue to trust his or her internal hunger gauge.

When it comes to battling an eating disorder, the best advice I can offer is to nurture your independence by doing things that allow you to feel comfortable in your skin. You can achieve this by doing whatever it takes to improve your body image and create a stronger self-image. Striking out and creating your individuality can be very exciting. Not everyone wants to have a "cookie cutter" body like others because that would make for a pretty boring world.

So if you find your jeans are a little tight or you gain a couple of pounds, don't let it make you crazy. Eleanor Roosevelt once said,

> "No one can make you feel inferior
> without your consent."

Learning to validate your own self-esteem and body image and not looking to others to accomplish this can only improve your outlook and life. If you feel happy and beautiful and act happy and beautiful, people will see you that way. I promise!

CHAPTER 5

Doing an *inner* Makeover

> " *I have met many girls that love their body, but if they are considered heavy then there is a problem. Overweight is a very touchy word because it does not take many pounds for someone to be considered overweight for their height. It is really amazing how your height plays into it. Beauty is not about your body size but about the size of your heart.*
>
> **—ARIANNA, NEW YORK, NEW YORK** "

A lot of girls grow up watching beauty pageants, dreaming they'll someday be that beauty on stage, sashaying across the floor with their faultless fit body, their beautiful hair perfectly curled, waving from their elbow and wrist, waiting to hear they are about to be crowned the next Miss America.

I wasn't one of those girls.

But lots of girls I know were, which got me thinking.

When did life turn into a constant beauty pageant?

Why is it that we all feel the need to compete as if we were one of *those* girls?

Our looks are constantly being critiqued and compared with impossible standards of perfection. If we don't stop accepting this as the norm, then we will spend a lifetime being defined by our looks and what's on the outside, rather than by our actions, our intelligence, and our accomplishments.

By now I've made you aware that it is society and the media that place this giant emphasis on our looks and weight. Knowing this, you can now make a conscious decision to reject any negative messages you receive about your body and learn to make changes to *love* your beauty from the inside out. I don't mean stop watching your favorite reality TV shows altogether, just be more aware that what you're watching is not reality! It's a television show, and it's usually scripted and edited to make it more entertaining.

While I've given you lots of examples of outside influences that can impact your body image, it's time to take ownership of the most powerful authority over how you see yourself.

It's you!

When you get right down to it, you are the only thing that prevents yourself from feeling truly ***beautiful, valuable, and worthwhile.***

I know this seems like a lot to take in, but stop and think about it for a minute. Since most of us live in a world where outer beauty is given such importance, we actually believe that without it, we're not special, unique, important, or relevant.

I call this BS!

If you want to change how you view yourself, you must first change how you see things. You have to rethink everything you've based your opinions on up to this point. You have to let go of society's expectations, family expectations, media expectations—even your own expectations—so that you can start the process all over again, but this time with a clean slate. If you do, the opportunities and possibilities are endless!

So here it is . . . beauty comes in many forms, which

means a variety of shapes, sizes, ages, colors, and so on. One of the most radical changes you can make is to start right now, this very moment, loving your own unique beauty—inside and out. I mean truly embrace it for all that it is and is not.

I know, you're probably asking yourself, how can I do this? It's not as hard as you might think. You have to change your thought process from negative to positive, which in turn changes your perception and how you see things.

SECRET . . . THE POWER OF POSITIVE.

8 What do you need to accept about your body to begin the process of letting go of your negative thoughts and turning them into positive ones? If you need help answering this question, go back to chapter 1 and reread your answers to the body image quiz on page 55.

We all love makeovers. Who hasn't caught themselves mesmerized while watching *America's Next Top Model* and a lot of other makeover shows? You see these totally frumpy women come out, and then they are whisked away by a team of experts who show them how to look ten years younger and twenty pounds thinner, give them a new haircut and a new wardrobe, and *voilà!* They're new women. These makeovers are nothing short of amazing. (By the way, I always wonder if in a month or a year from now they're still keeping up their amazing new look. I kind of doubt it.) Well, girls, it is time to do a makeover on you. I am not talking about one on the outside—nope. This one is all about redoing the inside—the way you think, feel, and act. And I promise, this is a makeover that will last!

The *Power* **of Our** *Words*

> " *Words have a magical power. They can bring either the greatest happiness or deepest despair; they can transfer knowledge from teacher to student.* —SIGMUND FREUD "

There's an old saying that goes "sticks and stones may break my bones, but names can never hurt me." I have always found this to be totally absurd because **words can and do hurt,** often way more than a punch in the arm. All of us have probably been made fun of in our lives, and if it hasn't happened to you yet, consider yourself blessed. When someone calls us names or makes fun of us, we might laugh it off in front of our friends to make it seem like we don't care, but when we go back home at the end of the day, that name we were called is probably still bothering us. We have all been hurt, and trust me, this is not only okay, it is actually a good thing to be conscious of. We should all be aware that the tongue is one of the wickedest and most powerful weapons known to man. Our words have the ability to tear us down or build us up. Unfortunately, most people use their words to lash out, hurt, destroy, and defame others, and worse, themselves. Hurtful words cut deep and are hardly ever forgotten. This is a form of verbal abuse, and it's not okay, whether it comes from parents, teachers, your boyfriend, or girlfriends. You can even call it bullying, but either way, it is all wrong.

When I was in grade school, some of the kids in my class used to call me "Bucked Tooth Beaver" because I had two big and white front teeth that stuck out a bit. Whenever I'd hear them call me that, I felt really embarrassed, so much so that I stopped smiling, which was really unusual for me. I became hyperaware of my teeth and did everything I could to hide them. I even practiced in front of the mirror how to smile with my lips closed. Name-calling is often more hurtful than someone punching you in the stomach, and it's not a fleeting pain—those words can last your whole life.

As I got older, it occurred to me that people say hurtful things because they have built-up anger, regret, or self-image problems that have nothing to do with you.

Mean Girls

We have all heard of or watched the famous movie *Mean Girls*, where Lindsay Lohan plays a character who is the new kid in town. She enters a new school where she doesn't seem to fit in to any of the cliques. She decides she needs to change herself to be accepted, so she can join the popular girls, called "the Plastics." The head girl in that clique is considered the queen bee in high school. She is pretty, thin, rich, and dates the most popular boy. While most of the kids in school loathe the queen bee, they are all too afraid of her to confront how poorly she treats everyone.

This movie got me thinking about the way girls treat one another. Girls are so mean to girls, when in reality we should be one another's number one supporters. We already feel like we have to dress up and be judged by the guys in our lives, so why do we find it necessary to do the same thing to our fellow girls? Why is it that we want to tear one another down instead of building one another up? Sadly, most girls are fiercely competitive and are too afraid to embrace someone who threatens their existence, their self-worth. The hurtful things girls say about one another, either behind their backs or to someone's face, only serve to degrade our gender.

You've got to have a posse of girlfriends who are in your life to help you celebrate yourself. As Maya Angelou once said, "Surround yourself with people who bring out the best in you." Do exactly that, and you'll feel great!

Dr. Christiane Northrup shared with me that she and her daughters are all graduates of Mama Gena's School of Womanly Arts, in New York City. The school teaches women of all ages how to use their power of pleasure to have their way with the world. In the class, 250 women get together once a month for four months and learn to celebrate who they are. Instead of tearing one another down, these women support one another. They compliment each other; they highlight the great points we as women all have.

Part of the curriculum is learning how to brag about

yourself. Instead of saying "My legs are chubby," they say, "My legs are really hot." You'll be amazed at how quickly your girlfriends will jump on the bandwagon, supporting your positive and self-esteem-building statements by commenting too. They'll say, "Yeah, your legs are hot!" Or, "You look fierce in that dress."

Pay a compliment to yourself and watch how others follow.

Trust me!

It may seem weird and feel strange to compliment yourself, but you deserve it! Go on and give it a shot! If you start complimenting yourself, so will other people.

Once I graduated high school and started college, a lot of the high school, queen bee drama was left behind. I chose my friends very carefully. Girls will be girls, so the likelihood is that you will deal with catty women for the rest of your

SECRET . . . PAY SOMEONE A COMPLIMENT TODAY.

9 If you see a woman who looks fabulous, tell her! That small act will uplift her for the rest of the day. It will make you feel really good too. Doing this creates what Dr. Christiane Northrup refers to as "an epidemic of health," because you are spreading smiles, which releases feel-good chemicals in our brain that make us feel better about ourselves. Believe it or not, these chemicals are the same ones that are released when you eat chocolate or something sweet. Isn't giving away a compliment a much healthier alternative to eating chocolate?

life. The best advice I can offer is for you to ask yourself what is going on in her life. What is making her so insecure that she has to lash out and verbally whip someone else or talk behind a person's back, to make her feel better about herself? If you can take a step back and see what is really going on, you will discover that most mean girls are insecure and so desperately afraid that no one will like them the way they really are, that they would rather point a finger at someone else before someone points a finger at them. They would rather make you an enemy first before you see them for who they really are.

My advice to you is to surround yourself with girlfriends who support you and love you and make you feel better about yourself. Life is too short to let a negative friend invade it!

Turn That Frown Upside Down—
Turning Negative Self-Talk into *Positive*

Words are extremely powerful. They can make us laugh, cry, think, or act. They can create or destroy. They can motivate you to leap into action or keep you from ever getting off the couch. The power of words is the biggest reason I can offer about why you should think before you speak. Once those words are spoken, they're awfully hard to take back. This is especially true when it comes to what we say to ourselves.

Are your thoughts and word choices building you up or tearing you down? **Most people who think negative thoughts aren't even aware they're doing it.**

Have you ever caught yourself saying anything like this?

1. I'm fat.
2. I can't . . .
3. I'm ugly.
4. I'm miserable, unhappy, discontent.
5. Why does this keep happening to me?
6. I'm so stupid/I'm an idiot.
7. I don't fit in.
8. No one likes me.

The list is never ending. These are all examples of what experts refer to as *negative self-talk*.

Did you know that the human mind has tens of thousands of thoughts a day? Experts estimate that the range is somewhere between 50,000 and 70,000!

And guess what?

Most of them are negative.

We all battle those thoughts every single day. We spend the bulk of our time thinking thoughts that lead to feelings of doubt, lack, limitation, worry, and fear, just to name a few. And to make matters worse, we continue having these same thoughts over and over, like they're playing on some type of continuous loop in our minds. The mind appears to be naturally wired to go to bad places.

What's up with that type of thinking?

What do you really gain?

From my own experiences, the answer is pretty simple —nothing!

Every thought you have creates a message in your brain. If you keep feeding yourself negative information, you will never be able to break the cycle. The goal is to learn ways to control your internal communication that will ultimately limit negativity in your life. Unless you change your internal program by turning your negative thoughts into positive ones, you cannot change your old thought patterns.

Sounds hard, right?

It is, but it's not impossible.

Most people have a hard time giving up negative thinking because it is the way we have programmed our brains to think. That's why it is a habit that's very hard to break. If you want to change your negative thought patterns, you have to learn to reduce negativity in your life. The easiest and first step is to stop talking negatively about you!

Tell yourself every morning that you're going to think positive thoughts today. If you make a real effort, I promise that pretty soon the negative voice in your head will start to fade away.

> ## SECRET . . . UNLIMITED POTENTIAL.
>
> **10** According to success coach Tom Ferry, the secret to giving up negative self-talk is more about awareness than effort. Once you learn to reject those self-limiting beliefs, they lose all of their power over you. When you change your self-talk, you change your self-concept, which in the process unleashes all of your true unlimited potential.

Building Up Your *Self-Esteem* and Creating a *Positive Body Image* for You!

Most experts agree that a negative body image is directly related to negative self-esteem. Self-esteem is based on judgments we all have about ourselves. It measures how much you respect yourself, how you feel about how you look, how you feel about your accomplishments, how loved you feel, and how you think of yourself as a person. The way you see yourself impacts every part of your life. If you've only been feeding your brain negative messages, then you have been stunting your level of self-esteem. Research has shown that the higher your self-esteem, the happier you are, the more confidence you have, and the better you feel about all areas of your life. Think of it like this: If you could have the ability to receive compliments every day or criticisms, which would you choose? You'd probably go for the compliments, right? I know I would!

Criticism is a part of all of our lives. Since we are our own worst critics, the negative things we tell ourselves are equally as powerful as the criticism we often hear from others. Sometimes criticism comes in the form of "constructive" criticism, meaning its intent is to help you improve on something for your own good, while other times it is meant to be hurtful. Either way, both leave you feeling imperfect.

Every summer, my family congregates on Cape Cod. It's a time for my cousins, aunts, uncles, and other loved ones to get together and bond. "Bonding" in my family sometimes means hearing the truth, whether you want to or not.

I went through a period where I dyed my hair darker and darker until it was finally a purplish shade of jet-black. Whenever I'd go back to the salon to get it dyed, the stylists pleaded with me to stop, that my hair was getting weird-looking. But I kept doing it anyway—it was my form of self-expression. My brothers made fun of my jet-black hair, which was usually the start of some family feud. I didn't like being criticized in general, but I especially didn't like it coming from my siblings or relatives.

As if my funky hair wasn't enough to deal with, I also had several piercings—nothing radical, just a bunch of earrings in both ears and the belly button ring that lasted two days until my mother saw it and threatened to ground me if it wasn't out by the morning. My cousins couldn't figure out what it all meant, and the fact that most of them are very conservative didn't help my situation at all. In fact, a few didn't understand why I even had pierced ears in the first place.

I didn't choose to do these things strictly as an act of rebellion. It was more about striking out and making a statement about my independence and individuality. My parents were really good about letting me experiment with my various "phases." They were smart enough to choose their battles wisely. They didn't *love* every risk I took with my appearance, but if none of those decisions were inherently dangerous, it was okay. I wasn't hurting anyone else or myself, and I would have to live with the consequences of those choices, so they never said a word when it came to my hair or my fashion hits and misses.

When we headed to the East Coast during the summers, however, I always felt a little like the black sheep in my conservative extended family, which in turn made me feel rather imperfect in that perfect Cape Cod setting.

It's kind of funny to think about because I felt totally "normal" when I was in Los Angeles among my friends who were also experimenting with different looks. My cousins ribbed me for my "unique" appearance, telling me I looked ridiculous and strange, which I probably did.

"What are you, goth?"

"Why are you wearing dark nail polish?"

"Why do you have so many earrings?"

"Are you angry?"

"What are you doing with your hair exactly?"

"Have you gone punk rock on us?"

The connection between how we think and how we appear is important for creating healthy self-esteem and a positive body image. I was completely comfortable with my hair color and ear piercings in my LA setting. But hearing the questions and criticism in Cape Cod made me feel insecure and lost. Our mental picture of our body is created by our thoughts, feelings, judgments, sensations, awareness, and behavior. A person develops a healthy body image when her feelings about her body are positive, full of **confidence and self-love.** These traits are essential if you want to care for your body and become comfortable with yourself.

Every year my mother hosts the annual California Women's Conference. Even though the event has been a success year after year, she still stresses herself out that it may not be the next time around. I've watched and listened as she psychs herself up in the days leading to the opening event. She literally stands in front of a mirror and tells herself:

"This is going to be a great Women's Conference. It's going to be amazing! Everyone will learn something!"

By doing this, my mom psychs herself up, sets high expectations for herself, and creates a self-belief that her conference will once again be a tremendously successful event.

6 THINGS
YOU CAN DO TO
build your self-image

1 Don't talk negatively about your weight or share your dissatisfaction with your own body. The more you belittle yourself, the more you will believe that it is okay to dislike your body. If you need to shed a few pounds, talk about it in terms of health rather than appearance. Losing weight is about being healthy and not just being thin.

2 You should never use the word *diet* even if you're on one. Choose phrases such as "getting healthier" or "getting in shape."

3 Don't use fad diets, pills, or other methods to quickly lose weight. The only way you should ever lose weight is by eating a healthy and balanced diet and exercising regularly. You need all of the nutritional benefits of eating healthfully, not to mention an understanding of the dangers you face by crash dieting.

4 Exercise! Get up and move. Begin a regular exercise plan and stick to it. Stay active and participate in physical activity to keep your mind and body in shape.

5 Don't compete with others. There is a natural tendency for girls to compete, but when it comes to your well-being, you're not doing yourself any favors. Girls will always compare their weight to their friends' weights. But a friend will always either be bigger or smaller than you. Either scenario has no upside.

6 The degradation of women doesn't exist only in our culture. It can happen right in your own home if you let it. Be kind to other women. Change starts with us.

How can you work on building your self-esteem?

Like all things worth doing, it takes time and practice. Verbal exercises like the one my mom does before her conference are a good start. You can begin each day in front of a mirror, setting goals for yourself and reminding yourself of all your positive attributes. Say you love your eyes, hair, hands, feet, body, breasts, booty, whatever, as long as you're not focusing on the areas that bother you. Remind yourself that you are a smart, courageous, loving, kind, and compassionate person. Think of the various things in your life that you should be grateful for, such as friends, relationships, family, and pets. Doing this will set you up for a day full of confidence, where you feel beautiful and get things done!

Now, try these next few steps to remind yourself what an amazing woman you are. I know it may feel weird, but just try it! Acting self-confident is the first step to feeling self-confident. So go ahead and smile, because people are attracted to happy, friendly people.

1. Instead of focusing on the negative things about your body, *focus on the things you like.* (Go back to the exercise on page 35 to remind yourself of what those are!)

2. You have to have a willingness to love yourself and *stop obsessing* over your perception of what's wrong. If you don't stop nitpicking, others won't realize how special you really are.

3. *Stop* reading magazines, surfing the Web, and watching television programs that don't make you feel good about yourself.

4. **_Exercise!_** This cannot be overstated. Positive feelings about our appearance develop as we take control of our health. Exercise has been proven to improve your mood, so get up and get moving!

5. **_Embrace yourself!_** Stop being your own worst critic. Give yourself the same break you'd give to others by not resorting to self-defeating mind chatter and statements.

6. **_Question_** the media's push for perfection. Stop asking what's wrong with you and start asking what's wrong with the media!

7. **_Quit dieting!_** Eating healthy, balanced meals is better for you.

8. **_Give compliments_** and learn to receive them by saying "Thank you" instead of "Really? Do you think so?" and "You're crazy! I look terrible" when someone says you look pretty, thin, vibrant, etc.

9. **_Don't judge_** people by how they look. Remember, you don't want to be judged either.

10. Accept you're a **_work in progress._**

11. **_Stop worrying_** about what others think of you. When you can let go of the opinions of others, you set yourself free from living up to or down to their expectations and will finally be able to meet your own.

12. **_Choose to change_** for yourself—not for anyone else, not even a boyfriend you're madly in love with! Do it for you!

13. **_Be an example_** for others by loving your body from the inside out.

CHAPTER 6

Eating for *Health*

> " *My mother was naturally tall, thin, and beautiful, while I was short and chubby. She put me on my first diet at nine.* —KIMBERLY M., ATLANTA, GEORGIA "

> " *My grandmother, who is fat, by the way, has no tact. She told me (at Thanksgiving no less, while we were eating pie!) that I only like fattening foods and that's why I'm not as thin as my cousin. At another point, she told me that I was a 'beautiful girl' but that I would be 'just that much more beautiful' if I 'lost a couple of pounds.' But she's excused, I suppose, because she's old.* —RACHEL, NEW YORK, NEW YORK "

173

If there was one word I would like to remove from the dictionary, it would be ***diet!*** This four-letter word plagues almost every girl I know—even those who don't need to lose weight. Some girls are perpetually on a diet and spend most of their life trying to get to that elusive weight or perfect size. ***That's no way to live!***

You may feel like now that your body is changing (or has changed) that you've gained weight. This may be true, but the likelihood is that you have also been making the wrong food choices along the way, which hasn't helped your bottom line. A lot of young girls keep eating exactly the same way they did before because their food intake didn't impact their weight back then like it does now. Suddenly, eating chips, cookies, Twinkies, and candy bars, and drinking soda matters because you will notice a significant weight gain. Your body is now processing things slower because your metabolism is changing. That is why this is a very difficult time for you to be dieting.

According to nutritionist Heather Bauer, the biggest mistake most girls make is trying to go lower in weight than their body's natural set point—the weight where your body is most naturally comfortable. And worse, girls are attempting to diet at too young an age. This is one of the most crucial times to eat a healthful and balanced diet because eating well at a young age sets you up for life.

When I was in my early teens, I started intensely riding horses and competing in equestrian events most every weekend, which gave me a high level of discipline and something to do every day after school. It also gave me a valid reason to stay thin. I'd go to horse shows that lasted all weekend, with my days sometimes starting at four-forty-five in the morning and ending as late as seven-thirty at night. It wasn't unusual for me to go all day without eating, especially when I was competing. My refusal to eat wasn't intentional; at least I didn't think so at the time. I just didn't like the way I felt after a meal. And if I rode my horse after eating, all I wanted to do was throw up. Diet Coke and Gatorade were the steadiest staples in my diet for most of my early teen years.

It didn't take long for my mom to notice my awful eating habits, especially by the time I hit high school. She began to notice more what I was eating, particularly at horse shows, where she was a constant fixture watching me compete. She never forced me to eat or made me feel like I was doing something wrong, which was a smart approach, because I was the type of kid who would have rebelled against anything I felt I had to do. Whenever someone said to me, "Are you sure you want to eat that doughnut?" I inevitably shoved the whole thing in my mouth as a way of saying, *"You're not the boss of me!"*

Knowing this, my mom would simply remind me that I needed to eat for energy and so I could be good at riding. She'd give me several logical reasons why eating was essential if I wanted to stay competitive. After all, though I was riding and jumping a three-thousand-pound horse, I barely weighed ninety pounds when I first started jumping and slightly over a hundred by the time I started high school. I was burning hundreds of calories with every round I competed in yet never refueled my body for energy, stamina, and strength. It was insane to believe I could keep my energy up without eating.

> *I started drinking Slim-Fasts for breakfast when I was in ninth grade. It started out as a convenience thing—I ran track and didn't have time in the morning to make breakfast. But then I started receiving compliments after I shed a few pounds, and the attention made me want to continue.*
>
> **—BETH, NEW YORK, NEW YORK**

> *The first time I ever self-imposed a 'weight-loss plan' was in the tenth grade. I was quite thin then, but the novelty of the concept struck me. I took Metabolife (a supplement that speeds up your metabolism) a few times a day. This diet lasted for about three days total. The pills made my heart beat at a rapid pace, and this scared me . . . so I stopped.*
>
> **—KATHRYN K., CINCINNATI, OHIO**

Your body is hungry for quality nutrients to keep up with your changing needs and to help you stay energized. The quality of the food you eat is substantially more important than the quantity, although it has to be said that overeating is never a good idea! Eating too much or choosing the wrong foods will always result in weight gain.

Dieting can be tricky, especially if you're experimenting with fad diets like Atkins, the South Beach Diet, or something more extreme, like the Master Cleanse or the cabbage soup diet. Following a weight-loss program that is designed for an adult doesn't take a teenager's maturing and changing nutritional needs into account. It is such a cool thing to have a healthy, young metabolism. Why would you want to alter that by going on a strict and regimented diet?

Here's the deal.

Many of you think you're doing your body good by counting calories, analyzing your carbohydrate and fat intake, and trying to keep your eating to the bare minimum. You probably think you are doing all of the right things to drop a few pounds or keep your weight stable, am I right?

Well, you're not!

All you're doing is causing yourself extra stress and math problems that have no real positive outcome anyway.

Heather Bauer sees a variety of young girls in her practice who go on strict diets at age thirteen, and by the time these girls are twenty-five they have the metabolism of an eighty-year-old! They've messed up their metabolism by too much extreme dieting and can no longer digest food like they should.

The eating habits we all have were most likely started in our childhood and will follow us for the rest of our lives, so it makes sense to develop healthy food habits early on. If you haven't developed good habits yet, your teenage years and early twenties are the most critical time for you to make a lifestyle choice where you learn to eat right, make better food choices, and give your body the nutrition it needs, because your body is still growing.

Guess what?

If you're among the majority of girls dieting, you are most likely depriving your body of essential vitamins, minerals, and nutrients it needs, now more than ever. Either you're making the absolute wrong choices or you are making no choices at all—eating whatever, whenever, without any thought about the impact that these food choices have on your body, weight, energy, stamina, awareness, and even your skin.

Throughout high school I tried one fad diet after

> *Sometimes I get frustrated because I think that no matter how much I work out or eat right, there are certain things (genetics, metabolism) that are out of my control and my body will always be a certain way. However, I always do feel better after a good workout, even though it's a mental difference, not a physical one, so I know I can always go do that and feel better.* **—RACHEL, NEW YORK, NEW YORK**

> *I try to avoid weighing myself. When I run and do yoga regularly, I feel good about my body. When I get into a sedentary pattern, less so.* —NINA, NEW YORK, NEW YORK

another. I went on a protein-only diet, a bad version of Atkins I made up; I did the Master Cleanse, where you are allowed to drink only a lemonade mixture, made with organic grade B maple syrup, fresh-squeezed lemon or lime juice, and cayenne pepper added to water for a minimum of ten days (I only lasted a day on this one!). While I did lose weight, the experience was disgusting! I tried all sorts of diets while watching my girlfriends experiment with their own. One friend made up the bubble gum diet, where she only ate bubble gum because, as she put it, "It's just like eating because you can put something in your mouth that is tasty, but then you can spit it out so you won't gain weight!" She was adamant she was going to lose weight and start a new diet craze. She was wrong on both counts.

There are really only three reasons you can be overweight:

1. You eat too much.
2. You don't work out.
3. You have a medical condition or have been taking medication that causes you to gain weight.

The health risks of being overweight, especially in your teens and twenties, are pretty dangerous if not debilitating. The more weight you carry around, the harder your body has to work to maintain its normal functions.

The possible risks for you include:

1. Heart disease
2. Diabetes
3. High blood pressure
4. Breathing problems
5. Brittle bones/osteoporosis

SECRET . . . GET MOVING!

11

The only safe and effective way to control your weight is to control the calories you eat and burn through exercise. So put on those sweats and start jogging or walking, bicycling, or anything else that gets you moving for at least thirty minutes a day.

It's hard to believe that you may be in danger of any or all of those five possibilities because they are conditions I would normally attach to someone who is older. Age isn't a factor when it comes to childhood obesity and its potentially dangerous side effects. If you don't act now, you will regret not taking charge of your health sooner.

Starting **Over**

Dieting is actually a habit. We choose particular foods, in precise and exact quantities that we eat only at specific times of the day. It is a habit you can break! You have the ability to actually stop making those choices, give up dieting, and start eating right. I wanted to know the skinny on creating this healthy lifestyle, so I asked Heather Bauer for some advice. She gave me her perfect formula when it comes to the food we eat.

**Smart food choices = staying full longer =
eating less = weight loss**

As Dr. Bauer describes it, "The formula is not rocket science. It's basic, simple, and has easy-to-follow strategies if you know how to make those smart food choices."

There have been many blessings and benefits to having Arnold Schwarzenegger as my dad, but it wasn't as much fun for us kids when he had to quickly get in shape for a movie. Once when I was younger, my dad came into our kitchen with a large garbage bag and emptied our entire freezer full of Popsicles, ice cream, and frozen dinners into the trash. He took everything bad or tempting in the house and threw it away. If he had to get in shape for a movie, we all suffered for it! If I was eating a muffin or pastry for breakfast, my dad would ask me if I knew how many calories were in the food I was eating and if I understood how many minutes it would take me to burn those calories in the gym. I'd rebel by stuffing the whole thing in my mouth, as if I didn't care. When I bring up this story to my dad about him tearing through the house and throwing out perfectly good food, we all laugh.

The strange thing about my dad's dramatic tactics isn't *what* he did—it's that he was actually right! If you're making a healthy change in your eating habits, experts actually recommend getting a fresh start by purging your fridge and replacing the old food choices with healthy alternatives. You don't have to throw away the food you just collected. You can always give it to a local food bank so you don't feel like you're being wasteful.

Starting over with the right foods sets you up for success. And if you can't totally cleanse your kitchen, you can, at the very least, reorganize the fridge, with healthy choices on two shelves, leaving the less healthy foods in the back or in drawers for family members who may not share your passion to eat healthfully (even though they should!). You can always ask your mom to hide the less healthy choices from you. Give her permission to put them away someplace where you won't be tempted to look. Like I always say, especially when it comes to food, "out of sight, out of mind."

HEALTHY FOODS
you can stock in your kitchen

A lot of girls want to eat healthfully, but they don't have a clue where to begin. I've put together a list that will help you get started. Ask your mom, dad, or whoever does the shopping for your family to consider buying some of these healthy foundation foods.

FREEZER
- Frozen fruits and vegetables
- Edamame
- Veggie burgers
- Dark chocolate

REFRIGERATOR
- Fresh fruits and vegetables
- Low-fat or nonfat dairy or dairy substitutes, including:
    - Skim, 1 percent, or soy milk
    - Margarine
    - Low-fat or nonfat yogurt
    - String cheese
    - Reduced-fat shredded or crumbled cheese
    - 1 percent or nonfat cottage cheese
- Chicken or turkey
- Fish
- Tofu
- And water!!

PANTRY

- Whole grains, including:
    - Instant brown rice
    - Whole wheat pasta
    - Whole grain wraps
    - Pita bread
    - Oatmeal
    - Whole grain dry cereal
    - Barley
    - Wild rice

STAY AWAY FROM

- White refined processed sugar
- Bagels
- Muffins
- Scones
- Pizza
- White pasta
- Candy
- High-fat foods
- Deep-fried foods
- Ice cream

SECRET . . . SMART SNACKING.

12 Fresh sliced turkey is a binge-safe food. No one ever overindulges on turkey. Can you imagine eating two pounds of turkey? Probably not! Except for the turkey we eat at Thanksgiving, at some point you will get sick of the taste long before you can overstuff yourself. Your body will automatically stop craving food once it has reached a feeling of being full. You can also keep fresh cut vegetables or fruits in your fridge to snack on.

Social Eating: *We All Do It!*

I don't know why, but it sure seems that most girls' social activity revolves around food.

"Meet me for coffee."

"Let's have lunch."

"I'll meet you in the cafeteria."

"Come over to my house. We can order a pizza."

Chances are, if you're eating out with friends, you're likely either going out to or bringing in takeout from a fast-food restaurant because it's quick and cheap. Which raises the fundamental problem that eating healthier means spending more money, so most people are eating lower quality food, especially with the downturn in the economy. Unfortunately, these cheap food choices are rarely the healthiest. One meal from a fast-food chain can equal an entire day's worth of calories, fat, and sodium. I don't like fast food enough to blow my entire day's worth of food eating one of their meals, but I know lots of people who do.

Just because I don't eat a lot of fast food doesn't mean that I cannot go with my friends when they want to eat out. I've learned to make smarter choices, which most of the chains now offer. You can ask for your sandwich to be prepared without sauce, mayonnaise, ketchup, and other dressings to save on unwanted calories. If you don't want to eat the sandwich dry, add mustard or ketchup, controlling how much you use by putting it on yourself.

SECRET ... OKAY TO INDULGE.

13

Save your indulgences for when you're eating out with friends. Believe it or not, you will likely make healthier choices when you are by yourself with no one else looking at what you're eating.

Another good tip for eating out is to *watch your portion size.* Don't supersize anything! Most of the portions are already more food than we need in a single serving. Sharing your meal is an easy way to divide and conquer the calories, so ask a friend to split that sandwich, burger, or pizza. A little trick my dad taught me is to eat my hamburgers without the buns! They taste much better and are healthier for you too.

Finally, *always try to substitute water for soda*—even if you're drinking diet soda. Recent government surveys reveal that sugared beverages are the number one source of calories in the American diet, representing 7 percent of the average person's caloric intake and 10 percent for children and teenagers! These calories are worse than useless. They're empty and contribute to a dietary total that is already too high. Water is an important element for effective weight loss. Since 65 percent of the human body is made up of water, it's important to flush out toxins and stay hydrated. Most experts tell you to drink sixty-four ounces (eight glasses) of water a day. Don't get bummed if you can't get that in. Aim to drink as much water as you can by replacing other options with water.

{
SECRET . . . H$_2$O TRICK.

14

Did you know that your body can
sometimes confuse thirst and hunger?
If you're hungry, try drinking at
least eight ounces of water before
grabbing a snack.
}

Breakfast **Is the** *Most Important* *Meal* **of the Day**

When I was a little girl, I saw an episode of *Sesame Street* about breakfast being the most important meal of the day. I never gave my morning meal much thought, but I decided to change all of that as I said good-bye to 2009. One of my New Year's resolutions for 2010 was to start eating breakfast. Simple, but not easy, at least not for me, because I am always on the go, go, go. My father always told me you can't get anything done in a day if you get up past five-thirty. My routine for years was to grab a breakfast bar, eat it on the run, and start my day. I thought I was making a healthy choice, but it turns out I was wrong.

Dr. Marie Savard explained to me that breakfast actually means "breaking a fast" in the morning. Your body needs something to jump-start your metabolism so it can begin to burn calories. I have always had a lot of get-up-and-go, finding it hard to relax or be sedentary, but I sometimes felt lethargic in the mornings and didn't know why. Dr. Savard advised me that choosing not to eat breakfast was a setup for eating more food later in the day, because my body would be starved. It also didn't give my body the fuel it needed to get my energy going. Once I discovered that eating breakfast helps my body burn more calories more efficiently throughout the day, I thought, "This may be the first New Year's resolution I actually keep!"

I'll let you in on a little secret. One of the reasons eating breakfast has been a challenge for me is that I am simply a bad cook. In fact, I only recently learned to cook different types of eggs for myself without burning them, which has now become my specialty. I can cook some basics, and I am slowly working my way up to something complicated, say chicken, but until I learn to broil or grill, oatmeal and micro-wavable meals are going to be a regular part of my diet.

As I am sure you can imagine, with a former Mr. Olympia and Mr. Universe for a dad, exercise has always been a big part of my life. Our family has enjoyed being physically active for as long as I can remember. There's simply no other way to take off weight than eating right and exercising. Working out is a key component in keeping off those un-wanted pounds. I grew up watching both my parents hit the gym.

I'm a girl who is all about routine. Having a routine helps me stay organized in all areas of my life. I usually hit the gym in the morning, which helps me start off my day with a lot of energy. Of course that sometimes changes, depending on my class schedule. Besides, having a set workout time keeps me occupied and out of the kitchen. Plus I actually like to work out. ***It's good for the mind, body, and soul.*** It gives you some much needed "you" time, and a time to clear your mind—something we all need and can benefit from.

I always feel better starting off my day with a rigorous workout. It gets my blood flowing and my brain switched on, and helps me feel completely ready for the rest of my day. Lots of research shows that working out releases endorphins, also known as the "feel good" chemicals in our bodies. Endorphins are a natural morphinelike substance that originates in our body and is released during long, continuous workouts, when the level of intensity is between moderate and high. It is sometimes referred to as "runner's high," although you can get this great feeling during any high-energy workout.

If you are ready to make a lifestyle change I highly encourage you to find something physical you enjoy doing. There are lots of options out there that are free and easy to access. You can bike, run, play tennis, Rollerblade, skate, or even use your Wii, which now has workout programs that get you physically involved by doing yoga, aerobics, weight training, and functional training. You can actually customize and personalize a workout program that targets your specific needs.

The most important thing is to get moving. So get up off the sofa, put down your fatty or sugary snack, and declare that today is the first day you will be in charge of your health, and then do something to prove it.

I love this tip,

which was given to me by nutritionist Heather Bauer. She suggests that you don't deprive yourself of an occasional indulgence—even when you are dieting. "I love ice cream, but I also want to avoid having large hips. If I want something sweet, I'll treat myself, but I won't overdo things. I'll eat a spoonful of Lovin' Scoopful or a small Pinkberry frozen yogurt to get my sugar fix, and then I'm less likely to eat an entire carton when I'm craving it!"

when it comes to losing weight, there is no quick fix. Remember, you are starting a complete change in lifestyle and not just aiming for weight loss alone.

SECRET . . . LOVE DOESN'T HURT.

15

Never ask your boyfriend (or husband) to tell you what they think about your weight unless you are mentally prepared to hear their honest answer. Trust me . . . brothers and boyfriends will voluntarily state their opinions about your weight whether you want to hear them or not. Once a guy I was dating told me I needed to start jogging with him because I was getting big. His comment didn't go over well with me, so instead of jogging with him I hightailed it home.

Let me just say a word here about boys and what's acceptable in relationships. Abuse, whether it is verbal, sexual, or physical, is a big issue for girls of all ages. You should know how you want to be treated in a relationship and make sure that happens. But if you are in your first relationship, you might not really know what is appropriate and what is not.

Any kind of physical abuse is unacceptable. You should leave immediately if you find yourself in a relationship that is abusive in any way. Love doesn't hurt. Someone who loves you doesn't hit or constantly berate and belittle you. That behavior is a sign not of love but that you are in an abusive relationship.

Everyone's relationships are different, but the one thing that we all have in common is that little voice in our heads telling us when something doesn't sound or feel right. I remember in one of my first relationships, I wasn't aware of what was considered appropriate or the "right way" for my boyfriend to be speaking to me. It took a while for me to realize that the way my boyfriend talked to and treated me wasn't acceptable. His words were abusive and made me feel terrible about myself. When I finally realized the way he spoke to me wasn't okay, I told him so. I said that I deserved to be respected and treated with kindness.

At some point most of us will probably feel stuck in an unhealthy relationship. The hardest thing to overcome is being able to recognize the situation for what it is, and then make sure it changes.

There are abuse hotlines that state what a healthy relationship is and is not. If you suspect you're in an unhealthy situation and need help to get out, look up your local abuse hotline for free and anonymous advice.

A healthy relationship should not make you afraid. It should make you feel valued, respected, seen, and cared for.

It's important to know that you cannot rescue a boy, especially someone who is hurting you. A boy doesn't love you when he abuses you. Many young girls unfortunately think they can change a guy and save him.

You can't.

And besides, it's not your job.

Getting your own life on track is hard enough without having the added responsibility of trying to help someone who is hurting you.

If you can relate to this "savior" mentality or have a boyfriend, friend, parent, or even a teacher treating you without respect and unkindly, make sure you let them know how you feel and demand that they change their actions. Listen to your gut. It is usually right.

SECRET . . . R.E.S.P.E.C.T.

16

It's a good thing to have a cool, kind gentleman as a boyfriend. But a guy who thinks he's cool because he can put people down is not the kind of guy you want in your life. Demand to be treated respectfully in your relationship from the beginning. If you don't, you will likely never earn his respect later on. Guys may call you a bitch because of it, but you're right to expect to be treated that way.

FOR MOMS ONLY

If you have a son, make sure to talk to him about the importance of being kind to girls. Make sure he knows what is and isn't acceptable behavior. My mom constantly tells my brothers how important it is that they be kind to their sisters and their female friends. Boys need to know that they can be kind and nice and cool all at the same time. This is really important and needs to be reinforced by the men in boys' lives too.

It's also vital to talk to your son about the word *no.* Teach him that when a girl says no, he has to stop, no matter what. Explain that he can't push her into doing something just because he wants to. *No* means **NO!**

The *Freshman* Fifteen

You've heard the rumors, the myths, the stories. The pretty girl from your school goes off to college thin as a rail and comes home virtually unrecognizable. She gained so much weight, she looked like she was wearing a balloon under her skin!

Is she suffering from some horrible disease?

No!

It's the dreaded freshman fifteen! (Cue music from *Jaws*. . . .)

Every girl who attends college or someday even hopes to needs to read this section of my book—over and over until you get that the freshman fifteen is a choice. It's a choice that can establish a pattern of weight gain that could become problematic if it continues.

When I started my freshman year of college at USC, everything was new, even though my school was only thirty minutes away from my parents' house. For the first time in my life, I was able to make decisions about everything. Where I lived,

FACT

A 2003 Cornell University study found that students put on an average of fifteen pounds between the time they leave high school and the end of their first year of college. The same study found that first-year college students put on approximately four pounds within their first three months away at school. That is eleven times higher than the expected weight gain for a typical seventeen- to eighteen-year-old and nearly twenty times the weight gain of the average adult.

who I lived with, when I went to class, when I ate, which foods I ate, when I studied, when I went out with friends, when to sleep in, just to name a few. College is a time of new beginnings. For many girls, it is definitely the first time they're truly on their own. If you were raised to be independent and self-sufficient, you will thrive in this environment. If you haven't quite got the skills to be independent yet, you will find this time a challenge.

There are many life changes for students entering their first year of college. Your freshman year may be the first time some of you are out from under your parents' control. It's like the first time being on vacation away from them. This new-found freedom, along with late-night munchies and un-healthful food choices at the cafeteria, all contribute to the onset of the dreaded freshman fifteen.

Budgeting time to exercise is only part of the equation. The foods you eat are the other. One of the biggest and most confusing issues for girls is how to manage food choices. For many students, college is synonymous with staying up late and experimenting with alcohol or drugs for the first time, which means eating lots of pizza and drinking beer, or other calorie-laden cocktails. Woo hoo! Party time!

But here's the thing.

All of those late nights, hearty cafeteria breakfasts on the go, bagels, fast-food breaks, greasy foods, french fries, pizza, and booze are the reasons you will pack on the pounds. Period. End of story. You don't have to give up having fun to avoid gaining this unwanted weight. Just make smarter, healthier choices for breakfast and lunch. Even if you're not hungry in the morning, get in the habit of grabbing a granola bar, a bowl of oatmeal, a yogurt, or a banana before your first class. This will get your metabolism started earlier, which will help you burn calories more efficiently throughout your day. Another helpful tip is to **drink more water** throughout your day. A lot of girls drink coffee or diet soda all day long, thinking this is a good alternative to eating. But it isn't. Diet soda and coffee dehydrate us. Water helps keep us strong and healthy by boosting our immune systems, something that can be vital for a sleep-deprived college student. When you consume too much caffeine, it can impact your sleep, which can affect your focus and concentration.

According to Dr. Marie Savard, two recent observational studies have shown that drinking as little as one diet soda a day increases by 40 percent your chances of developing metabolic syndrome, which is your risk of developing belly fat, diabetes, heart disease, and other ailments as you get older. Artificial sweeteners are addictive and can reset your brain to think it is being satisfied by the sweet taste without all of the calories. The problem here is that your body actually loses its ability to metabolize other sugars. So when you eat something sweet later on, your body thinks there are no calories coming with that taste, so it won't rev up your metabolism to burn those calories, which means you will gain weight. So the next time you reach for your diet soda or put an artificial sweetener in your coffee, thinking you're making the healthier choice, think again. Why not replace that drink with plain old-fashioned

SECRET . . . 17

HERE ARE FIVE EASY TIPS TO HELP YOU AVOID THE DREADED FRESHMAN FIFTEEN.

1. Avoid eating a heavy breakfast. Choose oatmeal over bagels, fresh fruit over a Danish or muffins. Limit eggs to a couple of days a week unless you're eating egg whites only, and avoid breakfast meats, including bacon, sausage, and ham.

2. Ask for all sauces, condiments, dressings, and toppings to be on the side—this way, you control the number of extra calories these add to a meal.

3. Skip cream-based soups and sauces. Choose tomato-based sauce over Alfredo and chicken-, beef- or vegetable-based stock soups over the heartier chowders.

4. If you want something sweet at the end of your meal, choose fresh fruit or frozen yogurt. Make dessert a treat—allow yourself to have it one night a week. I know, easier said than done, but you'll thank me for this one later!

5. Avoid late-night eating and drinking. Most likely you are not really hungry when someone says "Let's order a pizza" at midnight. You're either bored or wasted. These are never good times to make smart decisions about food. It's what I refer to as mindless eating, commonly done simply out of boredom. You eat without thinking about what you're consuming. If you are watching your weight, you will always regret this decision the morning after.

water or my personal favorite, sparkling water? It's healthier and cheaper!

Okay.

I know.

We are all aware that fast food isn't our friend, but the truth remains that most people will continue eating it—and loving every bite. Today more than ever, as the economy is still trying to recover, we all still want to eat out, but we don't want to spend a lot of money, especially if you're a college student like me. While I don't think eating fast food is necessarily healthful or good for your waistline, I humbly admit that I will occasionally indulge. The bottom line when watching your waistline, however, is that fast food should really be avoided like the plague. There are some healthier choices you can find among the fat- and carbohydrate-laden meals generally offered, especially at the chain restaurants, but the truth is, it's hard to resist the fries and shakes. Keep yourself safe by trying to stay out of these restaurants altogether, or at the very least, limit the number of times you eat there to no more than once a month.

FACT

According to recent studies, one-third of all children in the United States are overweight or clinically obese.

CHAPTER 7

Loving Your Inner and Outer Beauty

SECRET . . . YOU ARE BEAUTIFUL.

18

According to a 2009 *Glamour* body image survey, women under thirty are now 22 percent more likely to say they are happy with their shape than older women are. Historically, younger women have struggled most with insecurity. Women are finding their confidence sooner, thanks to recent education efforts and a realization that all body shapes and sizes are beautiful.

> " *I have never compared myself to anyone else, let alone to people in a magazine; my weight issues are only my views of myself. I used to think about my weight all the time. Through therapy, I have learned to manage that, and food is not work, it is something I should love. I love my body now.*
>
> **—ARIANNA, NEW YORK, NEW YORK** "

My parents always told me that I didn't have to act a certain way or change who I am in order to be accepted by others. They have always been true advocates for helping me embrace my individuality and uniqueness and learn to love myself for who I am. I spent some years being miserable, hating my body without ever giving myself a break. I now know that the focus shouldn't be on our bodies, it should be on our brains, what our minds can accomplish and what we put forward in the world. What your body does is far more relevant than how your body appears. Don't ever be worried about people judging you based on what they see on the outside. If they choose to make a fast judgment about you and make the decision not to get to know you first, they are most likely not worth your time and not worth having in your life.

I will never forget waking up early one morning in March 2009 to a headline in the *Los Angeles Times* reporting that talk show host Laura Ingraham had mocked former presidential candidate John McCain's daughter Meghan as "just another Valley Girl gone awry." According to the article, Ingraham had joked that McCain didn't get a role on MTV's *The Real World* because "they don't like plus-sized models. They only like women who look a certain way." I was shocked that she could say that about another woman! We are all supposed to be on the same team, and what had Meghan ever done to Laura Ingraham to cause her to lash out like that?

I have met Meghan and not only like her but also admire her very much. I could only imagine how Laura Ingraham's comments must have hurt her. It felt like a high school mean girl mockery all over again, only this time it was between two adult women. I was frustrated by the story and felt just awful for Meghan.

A couple of days later, I read Meghan McCain's response, which I thought was absolutely perfect! She said, "I have been teased about my weight and body figure since I was in middle school, and I decided a very long time ago to embrace what God gave me and live my life positively, attempting to set an example for other girls who may suffer from body image issues. I have nothing to hide; I am a size eight and fluctuated up to a size ten during my father's campaign. I feel it is ridiculous to have this conversation because I am not overweight in the least and have a natural body weight."

"You go, girl!" I thought.

Later that day, Meghan appeared on *The View*, where she quoted Tyra Banks, who faced her own humiliating headlines in early 2007 after two tabloids ran unflattering photos of her in a bathing suit with horrifying headlines that screamed "America's Next Top Waddle" and "Tyra Porkchop." Fed up by the media's scrutiny of her fluctuating weight, Tyra appeared in a bathing suit on her talk show and famously announced that her critics could "kiss my fat ass!" McCain told the ladies of *The View* that was *exactly* how she felt about her critics too.

Now, I am not one of those girls who spends tons of time on Facebook or Twitter, but I heard that Meghan had a few good responses on Twitter that assured all of her curvy girls she had their backs. The first one was clear. "To all the curvy girls out there, don't let anyone make you feel bad about your body. I love my curves and you should love yours too."

"Woo hoo!" I thought. "Good for her!" A response like hers was long overdue, where someone stood up for the curvy girls and admitted they are comfortable with their body size, regardless of what anyone else thinks. Clearly she had gotten over her body image issues long before her exchange with Laura Ingraham. At age twenty-four, she had learned not only to embrace the body she has, but also to love it, and she seemed to be screaming it from the mountaintops. I really admire her for being so vocal about her weight and dismissing others' negative comments about her!

Coming from a political family on both sides, I was aghast at the need of any member of the media to attack someone for their appearance. Granted, I grew up in a home where opinions were not only welcomed but often required.

And though I believe that everyone has a right to say what is on their mind, I found it unconscionable that Laura Ingraham would choose to verbally attack another woman not because of her views but because of her weight. In my opinion, she not only offended most women with her cattiness, but also singlehandedly reinforced the media onslaught of messages that how we look is more important than who we are.

Sadly, Meghan isn't alone in being singled out because of her weight. There is a long list of powerful and influential women such as Oprah Winfrey, Hillary Clinton, Mrs. Obama, and talented entertainers including Tyra Banks, Jessica Simpson, and Kelly Clarkson who have all fallen victim to this type of criticism. If they are still being judged for their weight despite all of the good things they've done in this world, who among us is safe from that way of thinking?

Tyra Banks has done so much to promote women loving their bodies. She readily admits to topping the scale at 164 pounds, which is thirty pounds more than her usual weight on her five-foot-ten-inch body. She also appeared on her fifth season premiere of *The Tyra Show* with no wig, extensions, or weave. Her hair was natural, as it is every day off camera. She did this to show other women who may have insecurities about their hair and various other parts of their body that they are not alone. Tyra has publicly announced her desire to help redefine the emotional issue of beauty women have, both from within and without. I admire her efforts and respect her bravery.

Any way you look at her, Tyra is a beautiful woman who has made millions of dollars with the body she has. Interestingly, Tyra's weight gain translated into higher numbers for both her talk show and *America's Next Top Model*, which she hosts. Perhaps her curvy figure is more appealing to her audience. Maybe it makes her more "real" to them. She feels good about her curves and imperfections—her booty, breasts, thighs—she embraces it all.

Tyra remained over 160 pounds for nearly two years after she famously told the world to "kiss her fat ass." She began to have severe stomachaches and enlisted the help of nutritionist Heather Bauer, who I talked to at length for this book. Heather helped Tyra regain control over her eating and taught her to make healthful choices, which in turn helped her to lose her excess weight—not to get skinny, but to get healthy. When she began eating right and making the right food choices, her stomachaches disappeared.

After all we have done to help promote equality for women in our society, **why is a woman's weight still an issue?** To me, a girl is beautiful when she loves herself. She is sexy when she radiates confidence. If you have self-love and confidence, you have the world on a string. Happiness and joy will surround you. When was the last time you heard someone say that a smile is disgusting? No one ever described a smile as "fat" or "ugly." It's just impossible!

So many girls have the wrong idea when it comes to what sexy and beautiful really are. Although "sexy" is something different to everyone, I feel *a woman is sexiest when she is totally comfortable with herself.* She isn't ashamed, embarrassed, or full of angst about how she looks or what other people think about her. So many girls work hard at trying to look good on the outside when, in fact, they should be working on the inside.

Both of my parents set the bar pretty high when it came to expectations, accomplishments, and creating independence. My mother gave me constant reassurance and guidance and led by example, while my father taught me the meaning of perseverance and determination. My parents helped me understand that what I saw as different about me is what made me special.

It wasn't until the start of my sophomore year at USC that I began hearing compliments from people more often.

I wasn't dressing any differently.

I hadn't lost weight.

I wasn't wearing my hair in a new style.

None of those things were eliciting praise.

I was happier—happier than I had ever been.

I was finally comfortable in my skin, where I was living, where I was going to school, and with all of my relationships. I had found self-love and an appreciation for my inner beauty, which radiated on the outside in every way as I moved through life. It wasn't an overnight transformation. It took a lot of self-awareness and hard work to finally get to the point where I was satisfied with my body and myself. And I'm still a work in progress!

My father once told me that I could achieve anything I wanted as long as I was willing to work hard to get it, and that is just what I did and will continue to do. He inspires me every day to follow in his footsteps by working hard and standing up for all that I believe in.

I hope I can play some small role in creating a positive message for all you young girls so that you'll understand that the size you wear has nothing to do with your self-worth and beauty or who you really are on the inside.

I read this poem by Maya Angelou a couple of years ago in a book I found in my mother's office. It has always stuck with me, which is why I want to share it with you.

Think of these words whenever you are feeling insecure, full of doubt, ugly, fat, stupid, or uncertain about life and your future.

PHENOMENAL WOMAN

by Maya Angelou

From her book *Phenomenal Woman*

Pretty women wonder where my secret lies.

I'm not cute or built to suit a fashion model's size

But when I start to tell them,

They think I'm telling lies.

I say,

It's in the reach of my arms

The span of my hips,

The stride of my step,

The curl of my lips.

I'm a woman

Phenomenally.

Phenomenal woman,

That's me.

If you or someone you know is suffering from an eating disorder, the following list of books will help guide you through the process. This list was created by the experts at the Walker Wellness Clinic in Dallas, Texas, a leading treatment facility specializing in eating disorders.

Books about Eating Disorders:
FOR ADULTS/PARENTS

1. *The Eating Disorders Sourcebook: A Comprehensive Guide to the Causes, Treatments, and Prevention of Eating Disorders* by Carolyn Costin.

211

2. *Learning to Be Me: My Twenty-Three-Year Battle with Bulimia* by Jocelyn Golden.

3. *Bulimia: A Guide to Recovery* by Lindsey Hall and Leigh Cohn.

4. *Life without Ed: How One Woman Declared Independence from Her Eating Disorder and How You Can Too* by Jenni Schaefer and Thom Rutledge.

5. *Eating in the Light of the Moon: How Women Can Transform Their Relationship with Food through Myths, Metaphors, and Storytelling* by Anita Johnston, PhD.

6. *Don't Diet, Live-It! Workbook: Healing Food, Weight and Body Issues* by Andrea LoBue and Marsea Marcus.

7. *The Body Image Workbook: An 8-Step Program for Learning to Like Your Looks* by Thomas Cash, PhD.

8. *The Overcoming Bulimia Workbook: Your Comprehensive, Step-by-Step Guide to Recovery* by Randi McCabe, PhD.

9. *Sensing the Self: Women's Recovery from Bulimia* by Sheila Reindl.

10. *Andrea's Voice: Silenced by Bulimia: Her Story and Her Mother's Journey through Grief toward Understanding* by Doris Smeltzer.

11. *Thin* by Lauren Greenfield.

12. *Wasted: A Memoir of Anorexia and Bulimia* by Marya Hornbacher.

13. *Diary of an Anorexic Girl* by Morgan Menzie.

14. *Gaining: The Truth about Life after Eating Disorders* by Aimee Liu.

15. *When Your Child Has an Eating Disorder: A Step-by-Step*

Workbook for Parents and Other Caregivers by Abigail Natenshon.

16. *Help Your Teenager Beat an Eating Disorder* by James Lock and Daniel Le Grange.

17. *Bulimia: A Guide for Family and Friends* by Roberta Sherman and Ron Thompson.

Books about Eating Disorders:
FOR CHILDREN/ADOLESCENTS

1. *Thin* by Lauren Greenfield.

2. *Wasted: A Memoir of Anorexia and Bulimia* by Marya Hornbacher.

3. *Diary of an Anorexic Girl* by Morgan Menzie.

4. *Learning to Be Me: My Twenty-Three-Year Battle with Bulimia* by Jocelyn Golden.

5. *Bulimia: A Guide to Recovery* by Lindsey Hall and Leigh Cohn.

6. *Life without Ed: How One Woman Declared Independence from Her Eating Disorder and How You Can Too* by Jenni Schaefer and Thom Rutledge.

7. *Eating in the Light of the Moon: How Women Can Transform Their Relationship with Food through Myths, Metaphors, and Storytelling* by Anita Johnston, PhD.

8. *Andrea's Voice: Silenced by Bulimia: Her Story and Her Mother's Journey through Grief toward Understanding* by Doris Smeltzer.

9. *Gaining: The Truth about Life after Eating Disorders* by Aimee Liu.

Acknowledgments

This book wouldn't have seen the light of day without the time, energy, organization, and intelligence of Laura Morton. She made my first experience a fun and memorable one—always answering my annoying questions, comments, and concerns with the love and support I needed.

I'm so grateful to all those I've come to think of as my Book Family—the whole team that helped make my dream come true. Jan Miller, Nena Medonia, Sarah Landis, Ellen Archer, Anne Sweeney, and all of the rest of the people at Hyperion, you have all been so supportive and loving throughout this entire process. Thank you for taking a chance on me and being as passionate about this important subject as I am. I love you all and this would not have been possible without all of you.

Thank you to all of my family and friends who helped me stay positive and upbeat throughout this journey. I especially thank my amazing mother, who took the time to be on every conference call, in every meeting, and always there to answer my questions. I so appreciate her advice, intelligence, and all the lessons, laughter, and love.

Thanks to those friends who took time to read several drafts of this book as well as offer encouragement and suggestions. Lindsay, who always gave me great advice and support from the moment this book was just the flicker of an idea; my fairy-godmother Nadine, whose wisdom and direction were always on target and appreciated; and Rachel, for your amazing and fun brainstorming for a title.